TAXATION SIMPLIFIED

MARCH BUDGET 2000

Clive Steward BA (Hons) FCA

95th Edition

2000

Annual updates of this book are available by subscription. Please see Standing Order form at the back of this book.

For a complete list of Management Books 2000 titles, visit our web-site on http://www.mb2000.com

First published in 2000
by Management Books 2000 Ltd
Cowcombe House
Cowcombe Hill
Chalford
Gloucestershire GL6 8HP
Tel: 01285-760722 Fax: 01285-760708
e-mail: MB2000@compuserve.com

Printed in Great Britain by Biddles, Guildford

British Library Cataloguing in Publication Data is available

ISBN 1-85252-326-3

CONTENTS

CHAPTER 4 BUSINESS TAXATION

CHAPTER 5 CAPITAL GAINS

CHAPTER 6 RENTS FROM PROPERTY

CHAPTER 7 MISCELLANEOUS MATTERS

CHAPTER 8 VALUE ADDED TAX

CHAPTER 9 INHERITANCE TAX

PREFACE TO THE 95th EDITION

Budgets used to be an event worth watching live on television. In times past, I had a note pad on my knees to jot down the allowances, tax rates and bands. This year, I had to wait to download the press releases from the Inland Revenue's website.

The big changes which started on 6 April 2000 were announced last year, e.g. abolition of MIRAS and the married couples' relief, and even the 1% cut in income tax.

Some anomolies from last year's budget have been corrected, namely the 19% band applying to Bank and Building Society interest and Capital Gains Tax.

The famous IR35 press release from March 1999 turned out to be a real tiger in attacking service companies (and partnerships). From 6 April 2000, all contracts have to be examined as to emplyment status. Beware of buying expensive, untested contracts from companies marketing off-the-shelf products. It could ultimately be very expensive! A key to the problem may be to incorporate the rights to substitute another person to do the work in the contract – but beware. It is the contract taken as a whole which points to employment or independence.

April 2000

Clive Steward BA (Hons) FCA
Chartered Accountant
Weston Zoyland, Somerset

SUMMARY OF RATES AND ALLOWANCES

A. RATES OF TAX

1. Income Tax (Net income after allowances)

1999/00		*2000/01*	
first £1 500	10%	first £1 520	10%
£1 501 to £28 000	23%	£1 521 to £28 400	22%
above £28 000	40%	above £28 400	40%

2. Corporation Tax

	1999/00		*2000/01*	
Starting Rate			£1 - £10 000	10%
Intermediate Profits			£10 000 - %50 000	22.5%
Small Company Rate	£1 - £300 000	20%	£50 000 - £300 000	20%
Intermediate Profits	£300 000 - £1 500 000	32.5%	£300 000 - £1,500 000	32.5%
Large Company Rate			£1,500 000+	30%

Small companies marginal relief fraction:	1/40	1/40

3. Capital Gains Tax

(a) Individuals

At marginal income tax rate (i.e. 10%, 20%, or 40%)

	1999/00	*2000/01*
Exemption limits:	£7 100	£7 200

(b) Companies

At the corporation tax rate.

(c) Trusts	*1999/00*	*2000/01*
Interest in possession trusts	34%	34%
Discretionary and A&M trusts	34%	34%
Exemption limits	£3 550	£3 600

4. Value Added Tax

	from 1.4.99	*from 1.4.00*
Registration limit	£51 000	£52 000
Deregistration limit	£49 000	£50 000

5. Inheritance Tax

	1999/00	*2000/01*
Exemption limit	£231 000	£234 000
Rate	40%	40%

B. PERSONAL ALLOWANCES

	1999/00 £	*2000/01* £
Personal allowance (each individual under 65)	4 335	4 385
Married couple's allowance, both under 65	1 970	nil
Additional personal allowance	1 970	nil
Widow's bereavement allowance*	1 970	2 000
Blind person's allowance	1 380	1 400
Maintenance payments	1 970	nil
Age allowances:		
(a) Age 65-74		
Personal allowance	5 720	5 790
Married couple's allowance*	5 125	5 185
(b) Age 75 and over		
Personal allowance	5 980	6 050
Married couple's allowance*	5 195	5 255
Income limit for age allowances	16 800	17 000

* Restricted to 10% from 1999/00.

CHAPTER 1

THE TAX SYSTEM

1.1 THE NEED TO UNDERSTAND THE SYSTEM

Why do we need to understand the system?

As citizens we should be able to discuss and, if necessary, criticise the government's measures for controlling the economy, in which taxation is an important factor, but we cannot sensibly do so without at least a basic understanding of the system. A more direct reason is that we are all entitled to arrange our affairs so that our personal tax liabilities are reduced to the legal minimum, and this, too, requires knowledge. Of equal importance is that we need to know how to avoid getting into financial difficulties in meeting the tax we are due to pay.

Many people are paying more tax than they need. This is not normally the fault of the tax offices, although mistakes do occur, and in simple cases the situation can be easily remedied by the individual concerned. In more complicated cases it is desirable to obtain expert advice, but it is necessary to know when to seek that advice.

1.2 WHY TAXES ARE NECESSARY

The purposes for which taxation is required may be summarised as follows:

- To pay for national expenditure on, for example, defence, government administration and interest on government borrowings; and for local expenditure such as for local services, health, education, welfare and interest on loans. National expenditure is met from taxes such as income tax, corporation tax, capital gains tax, and from customs and excise duties, such as value added tax, stamp duties and licence duties. Local expenditure is met from the rates, the council tax, and from grants from the central government.
- To enforce government financial policy, such as in controlling inflation and encouraging investment in industry.

The tax system is undoubtedly influenced by political motives, both in the wide and narrow sense. While we all naturally resent paying to the tax collector part of our hard-earned income, and feel that the burden on us individually is excessive, a principle of taxation is that it should be equitable as between one person and another. Everyone is, of course, entitled to their opinion as to the fairness of the system, but that opinion should be justified by knowledge.

1.3 LIABILITY TO TAX

All individuals resident in the United Kingdom of Great Britain and Northern Ireland are liable to pay income tax, capital gains tax and inheritance tax. Persons resident outside the UK so far as they derive income from UK sources are also liable to pay UK tax whether they are British subjects or not. Persons resident in the UK and receiving income from abroad are, in general, liable to UK tax on their overseas earnings, subject to certain reliefs and allowances. Companies are liable for corporation tax on income wherever it arises.

1.4 TAX RETURNS

All persons liable to UK taxation have the duty to complete Tax Returns and to submit them to the appropriate Inspector of Taxes. The form for a particular tax year shows the income received (including capital gains) and the applicable charges against income, for the previous tax year, as well as the allowances claimed for the current tax year. Inspectors of Taxes normally send out Self-assessment Tax Return forms early in each tax year, but they may not do so where all a taxpayer's income is covered by deduction of tax at source such as under the PAYE system for salaries and wages. (See **2.2** Self-Assessment). The 2000 tax return will have to be submitted to the Inland Revenue by 30.9.2000 if you wish the Inland Revenue to calculate your tax liability or by 31.1.01 if you calculate it yourself. Late submission will lead to a £100 penalty.

It is especially necessary to submit a Return to obtain all available tax allowances; to record investment income from shares, deposits and loans; to record sales and purchases of investments and other assets for capital gains; charges on income, such as mortgages and covenants, etc.; and where liability to higher rate tax may apply. It is particularly necessary to show untaxed income on the Return: for instance, interest not subject to deduction of tax at source, such as on many national savings and certain government securities. For individuals with small incomes the submission of a full return may result in a refund of excess tax suffered by deduction from income. Failure to make a Return, or the submission of a false or incorrect Return, does involve interest and penalties.

1.5 SERVICES FROM THE INLAND REVENUE

Information and advice on tax is available from numerous Tax Enquiry Centres, including Mobile Centres, but the Inland Revenue is not obliged to advise on how tax can be reduced and certainly not on how it can be evaded. A wide range of leaflets is available from Tax Offices. Following the Citizen's Charter of July 1991 improvements to the Inland Revenue service include: quicker and more informative replies to letters; simpler forms; 'phone-in' facilities; and generally a more personal service. Complaints may be made to an Adjudicator with regard to the manner in which the Inland Revenue has acted, but not on technical matters.

1.6 MINIMISING YOUR TAX

For the purpose of reducing your tax to the minimum legally payable you should ask yourself the following questions:

- Are you obtaining all the allowances to which you are entitled? – See Chapter 2, *Personal Taxation.* If not you may have failed to make the necessary returns to the Inspector of Taxes.
- Do you have a balance of income, after deducting allowances and charges, on which tax is payable? If not, you can reclaim from the Inland Revenue any excess tax deducted from interest, pensions, etc. Many married women, widows, divorcees, retired people and others with low income are liable for little if any tax and could recover some or all of the tax deducted at source from their income.
- If you are in business, even as a spare time venture, are you charging all allowable expenses in your business accounts? (See Chapter 4, *Tax on Business.*) Allowable expenses may include, for example, the business use of a car or reasonable fees or salaries paid to spouses or other relatives who assist in the business. Of particular importance are claims for capital allowances and the selection of starting dates.
- Have you arranged your financial affairs so as to reduce your tax liabilities? These arrangements could include, for instance, transfers of investments between husband and wife; life-time gifts to reduce inheritance tax; obtaining exemptions from capital gains tax; taking advantage of personal pensions and various tax-free investments. Reference should be made to the relevant chapters and sections of this book.

In this context we cannot over-emphasise the dangers of attempting to evade tax by, for example, deliberately omitting to declare income or falsifying the figures. Even many expertly drawn schemes of tax avoidance have turned out to be ineffective or are eventually overtaken by legislation. The penalties, both personal and monetary, can be severe, and the tax authorities have many sources of information.

In a complicated situation expert advice from a qualified accountant or solicitor specialising in the subject is necessary. The taxpayer should be wary of unqualified advisers or lounge-bar boasting! A great deal of help can be obtained from tax offices but it is not part of the duty of the officials to advise on tax minimisation.

In the more straightforward situations the information contained in the following pages will be sufficient for the taxpayer to manage his or her own tax affairs; it will also show when specialist advice is needed.

1.7 PROVIDING FOR PAYMENT

Most of the income tax due is collected by deduction from income. One example of this is the system for deducting tax from wages and salaries known as the Pay As You Earn system (PAYE). Under this system the amount of tax deducted is controlled by a code which is notified to the employer. If the code has been correctly allocated the amount of tax deducted will equal the amount due from the employee during the year. Another example is the deduction of tax at source from investment income such as interest. In this case the tax is deducted at a flat rate regardless of the person's tax liability.

Where income is received without being taxed at source, the tax due will generally be payable on 31 January in the year of assessment. However, where the tax is due on the profits of an individual's business there are three payment dates: 31 January in the tax year, and 31 July and 31 January following the tax year. The first two are payments on account, with a balancing payment (if any) on the 31 January immediately following the tax year concerned. The first two payments (on account) are estimates of the liability based on the actual liability of the previous tax year.

Obviously, if profits are rising the payments on account will not cover the total liability and will therefore leave a sum due for the balancing payment. If profits are falling you can apply to reduce the payments on account. Interest is payable if it subsequently turns out that you reduced these by too much.

Where tax has been deducted from investment income there will be a further liability to tax if the individual is liable to tax at the higher rate. In that case the tax will be payable on 31 January in the tax year following the tax year in which the income was received. (A tax year runs from 6 April to the following 5 April.)

Capital gains tax will also be payable on 31 January following the tax year in which the gain arose.

Companies are charged to corporation tax on all taxable income and gains. The assessment is based on the accounting period, and the tax is payable nine months after the end of that period.

Where tax is not paid on time the Collector of Taxes will issue demands, and will charge interest on tax paid late.

It is important to avoid financial difficulties when large demands for tax are received. This applies, in particular, to business profits, higher-rate income tax, and tax on untaxed interest. The remedy is to provide for the tax in advance through regular savings out of current income, but for that purpose it is necessary to know when the tax will become due and to be able to forecast the amount.

In too many cases people fail to make returns to the Inspector of Taxes, or make incorrect returns, of the income they receive. This particularly applies to occasional work and spare-time activities. This may be due to ignorance of the tax regulations or genuine mistakes, but the almost inevitable consequence is that tax demands on the undeclared income are received going back for six years, or longer where there is fraud. In the latter case severe penalties may be charged in addition to the tax due. Delay in payment will give rise to interest being charged in addition.

In 2000, the last date to notify the Inland Revenue of chargeability to tax for 1999/00 is 5 October 2000. Failure to do so will lead to a penalty of up to 100% of any tax paid late.

The self-assessment tax return will be issued in April 2000. Details of the accounts period ending in 1999/00 should be entered thereon. A sum of tax, based on the 1998/99 actual liability will already have been paid by 31 January 2000, and a similar sum is due on 31 July 2000. The tax return itself need not be returned to the Inland Revenue until 31 January 2001. On this date the balance of any tax due must be paid. This date should be kept to in order to avoid penalties and interest.

Collectors will not hesitate to take legal action to obtain long overdue tax. They may sue in the Courts, and distrain on the taxpayer's furniture and effects. Many people have been made bankrupt and companies liquidated for unpaid tax.

Certificates of Tax Deposit may be obtained to provide for the potential liability for income tax which is in dispute, thus avoiding an interest charge.

1.8 THE ADMINISTRATION OF THE SYSTEM

How taxation is authorised

The statutory authority for the imposition of taxation is contained in the following Acts of Parliament:

- Income and Corporation Taxes Act 1988 (a Consolidating Act).
- The Taxes Management Act 1970, covering the administration of taxation.
- The Provisional Collection of Taxes Act 1968, permitting the Budget proposals to be enforced until amended.
- The Capital Allowances Act 1990, providing for allowances on the acquisition of fixed assets by business instead of depreciation.
- Taxation of Chargeable Gains Act 1992.
- Value Added Tax Act 1994.
- Inheritance Tax Act 1984.

This legislation is amended by the annual (now July) and sometimes more frequent Finance Acts.

This enormous volume of legislation has to be interpreted by the Courts in an even greater volume of decided cases. In addition the Inland

Revenue from time to time publish 'concessions and practice notes', where the strict application of the law would be unjust or unworkable, and to indicate the methods they employ in particular situations.

Proposed amendments and additions to the current law and practice of taxation are presented to Parliament by the Chancellor of the Exchequer in his Budget Speech, usually in March of each year, sometimes more frequently. The 'Budget' is strictly a forecast of government income and expenditure for the coming year, and includes a review of the previous year's results.

The Budget proposals are set out in the Finance Bill which is then debated in Parliament. The provisions of the Finance Bill have immediate effect under the Provisional Collection of Taxes Act. Amendments made during the debate are incorporated in the Finance Act of the following July which may entail adjustments to the taxation provisionally imposed.

The fiscal year and the assessment year

The government accounting year for taxation purposes, or the 'fiscal year', ends on 5 April, and income tax assessments are made for each year ending on that date. There is a slight difference in the assessment year for corporation tax on limited companies and other corporate bodies and in these cases the 'financial year' ends on 31 March, thus conforming to the standard 'reference year' for such bodies under the Companies Acts.

For most of an individual's income – for example, income from employment – tax is calculated on the actual amount received in the year of assessment, at the rates of tax applicable to that year. For some income, notably the profits of a partnership or business in single ownership, the assessment year will normally cover the income shown by the accounts made up to a date in the year of assessment.

Corporate bodies, including limited companies, are charged to corporation tax on the taxable profits shown by their accounts for their accounting years. The rate of corporation tax applied is the rate applicable to the tax years covered by the accounting period. This is payable 9 months after the year end.

Organisation of the Inland Revenue

The general administration of the taxation system is the responsibility of the Board of the Inland Revenue, of which the members are called the 'Commissioners of Taxes'. Under the Board are (a) Inspectors of Taxes and (b) Collectors of Taxes. Inspectors have offices in tax districts which roughly correspond to the local authority areas but in some cases an Inspectorate is centralised to deal with a particular class of taxpayer, e.g. civil servants. Tax offices dealing with employments in London have been moved to provincial towns. Tax collection accounting has been computerised in Cumbernauld and Shipley.

Widespread reorganisation of Tax Offices began in January 1993. In many areas Taxpayer Service Offices combine the collection of tax with all but specialist work on assessments, personal reliefs and PAYE coding. Most taxpayers will, as a result, be saved the trouble of dealing with a number of tax offices. District Offices will be responsible for compliance with tax rules, audit functions and examining business accounts. Taxpayer Assistance Offices will assist the taxpayer in enquiries.

The inspectors have the responsibility of examining taxpayers' Returns of Income, issuing codes under PAYE, dealing with appeals, negotiating adjustments, and authorising repayments of tax. They have wide powers to require the production of documents and Inspectors can apply to a magistrate for the right to enter a taxpayer's premises.

The Collectors are in effect the cashiers of the Inland Revenue. They have the responsibility of ensuring collection from the taxpayer of the tax due under the assessment. They have no power to alter the assessment but they may in suitable cases agree to receive payment by instalments. If a taxpayer is finding difficulty in meeting his tax liability he or she would be well advised to discuss the problem with the Collector promptly and make a reasonable arrangement for payment. As with many things in life, if the taxpayer is up front, the collector is more likely to be flexible.

The General Commissioners of Taxes are persons of local repute, akin to magistrates, and not responsible to the Inland Revenue. Their function is to hear appeals by the taxpayer from the decision of the Inspector and to protect the interests of the taxpayer, subject to law. Alternatively, the taxpayer can appeal against a decision of the Inspector to the Special Commissioners. The latter are appointed by the Lord Chancellor and are experts in taxation law and practice. The General Commissioners are best qualified to deal with questions of local circumstances.

In May 1993 an independent Adjudicator was appointed to consider complaints from taxpayers, but will not deal with questions of law or valuations.

1.9 THE CATEGORIES OF TAX

Probably no one escapes the tax net in some form or another. We all suffer value added tax (VAT) on many purchases; most of us pay income tax, the council tax and National Insurance contributions; many are liable for capital gains tax. Companies pay corporation tax, capital gains tax, excise duties, VAT and business rates. For a full understanding of the system it is therefore desirable to consider all the taxes in which we may be involved.

Taxes are usually described as either direct or indirect and this classification is used below, although the distinction between the two categories is not always precise. Direct taxes are those charged directly on individuals, partnerships, trusts and corporate bodies and indirect taxes are of more general application.

(a) Direct taxes

Income tax. Charged on the total income of individuals, including their salaries, wages, pensions, fees and other remuneration; their dividends, interest and royalties; profits from business they operate alone or in partnership; and many other kinds of income, including for example, certain National Insurance benefits, alimony, etc. There are many reliefs and allowances deductible before taxable income is calculated. In 2000/01 a lower rate of 10% is payable on the first £1,520 of taxable income, a rate of 22% on income from £1 521 to £28 400, and a rate of 40% on income above £28 400. In 1999/00, the lower rate of 10% was payable on the first £1 500, with 23% on income from £1,521 to £28 000, and 40% thereafter.

Corporation tax. Payable by limited companies and other corporate bodies on their profits, at 30% for large companies and 20% (from 1 April 2000) for small companies. There is a starting rate of 10% on the first £10 000 increasing on a sliding scale to 20% at £50 000. For the year prior to this, the rates were also 30% and 20% respectively. The profits charged to corporation tax include both income and capital gains.

Capital gains tax. Payable by individuals (subject to many exemptions and reliefs) at marginal rates of tax on capital profits in excess of £7 200 in 2000/01 (£7 100 in 1999/00) made on the sale or disposal of assets.

Inheritance tax. Payable by the personal representatives of deceased persons on gifts made on death. The tax begins when total capital passing on death is over £234 000 in 2000/01 (£231 000 for 1999/00). The excess is taxed at 40%. There are many exemptions.

Rates and the Council Tax. A uniform business rate is payable by businesses on the assessed letting value of land and buildings, and the council tax is payable on domestic accommodation.

National Insurance contributions. Effectively a tax although not normally so regarded by the Government.

(b) Indirect taxes

Customs and Excise duties. Chargeable on certain dutiable goods imported and those produced in the UK, such as liquors and tobacco. Also various licence fees and stamp duties.

Value added tax (VAT). Administered by the Customs and Excise and chargeable on the sales value of goods and services, with many exemptions and zero-rated items. Payable through the whole chain of importers, producers and distributors, less tax on purchases, but ultimately borne by the consumer. Payable at 17½% by a business with a turnover of £52 000 from 1 April 2000 (previously £51 000 from 1 April 1999).

1.10 THE SCHEDULES

In addition to the more general regulations governing liability to income tax, as reviewed in preceding sections, more detailed rules apply to each of the taxpayer's different sources of income. These rules cover such matters as the basis of calculating the taxable income, and the method of assessment and payment. The rules are set out in six 'Schedules', A, C, D, E and F, to be found in the Taxes Act 1988. Some of these Schedules are further subdivided into a number of 'Cases'. Some Schedules and Cases are of little interest to the majority of taxpayers but they are all briefly described below with the aim of providing the reader with a broad view of the scope of taxes on income.

Schedule A covers income from property, i.e. rents less expenses – but not furnished holiday lets (see Schedule D Case vi below).

Schedule C provides for the taxation of interest, annuities and dividends paid in the UK out of public funds. The payments concerned may be made by the UK government, e.g. on government securities, or by a foreign government, public authority or institution. The assessment is made on the paying agent, e.g. the Bank of England or another bank. Thus, the ordinary taxpayer is not directly affected by this Schedule.

Schedule D. This Schedule embraces six subdivisions of income, or Cases:

- Case I deals with the profits of a trade or business (other than a business covered by Case II). Since this Case governs a very large proportion of total tax receipts it is dealt with in more detail later in this book.
- Case II applies to professions, e.g. lawyers, doctors and accountants, operating a sole business or in partnership, but if they are employed their salaries are assessed under Schedule E.
- Case III taxes interest from a loan; from government securities, such as 3½% War Loan and Defence Bonds, where tax is not deducted at source; co-operative society dividends; and other untaxed income.
- Case IV covers income from foreign securities, that is where the income is charged on some overseas asset, e.g. by a debenture.
- Case V covers income from foreign possessions and this phrase might cover business profits, dividends and rents from abroad.
- Case VI is the 'miscellaneous' Case which taxes income not falling within the scope of the other Schedules or Cases. Typical sources of income covered by this Case are dealings in futures, revision of 'venture capital' relief and development gains. Includes furnished holiday lets.

Schedule E. This is the important Schedule dealing with wages, salaries, bonuses, commissions, fees and benefits received in connection with an office or employment. Case I is the 'general' case applying to UK residents; Case II covers non-residents and individuals not ordinarily resident who are employed in the UK; and Case III covers residents in the UK receiving remuneration in the UK from outside the country; also tax on certain social security benefits.

Schedule F. This Schedule covers the income tax payable by a limited company or other corporate body and representing the tax 'imputed' to the dividend.

CHAPTER 2

PERSONAL TAXATION

2.1 ASSESSING THE LIABILITY

An individual is liable for income tax on the whole of his or her income which is chargeable to tax. That income may include, for example, remuneration from employment, business profit, rents from letting property or rooms, and income from investments. Very little income escapes the tax net. There may also be a liability for capital gains tax which is considered in Chapter 5.

From the gross income of a taxpayer from all sources certain charges on income are deductible, and these will be payments of an annual nature such as mortgage interest, maintenance payments under court orders, and for annuities and pensions. Gifts and living expenses are not allowable deductions. Personal reliefs and allowances are then deducted from the remaining amount, called 'total income', to produce a balance on which income tax is charged, the 'chargeable' income.

In 2000/01, income tax will be charged at the rate of 10% on the first £1 520 of chargeable income, 22% (the basic rate) on income from £1 521 to £28 400, and 40% (the 'higher rate') on income above £28 400; in 1999/00, the lower rate of 10% is applied to the first £1 500 of chargeable income, with £1 521 to £28,000 taxed at 23%, and income over £28 000 taxed at 40% (the higher rate).

For the purpose of calculating the higher rate payable, interest received and dividends to which the lower rate is 'imputed', must be 'grossed up'. Grossing up means calculating the amount of the interest or dividend by adding back tax which has been deducted.

The tax payable by an employed taxpayer, or pensioner, will normally be accounted for by PAYE deductions from the pay or occupational pension. However, the actual tax liability will often need recalculation after the end of the tax year leaving an amount underpaid or overpaid. The adjustments may be due, for instance, to incorrect codings for PAYE, and the correction of estimates, e.g. state pensions, income from property and investment income, not taxed at source.

Business profits made by the self-employed or partners are included, with all other sources and income, on the self-assessment tax return (see **2.2** below).

2.2 SELF-ASSESSMENT

Readers who require an overview of the new system of Self-Assessment, now in its fourth year, or would like specific guidance on how to complete their Self-Assessment Tax Return, please refer to the Appendix on page 137. This, taken with the Guide which accompanies the tax return, will take you through the maze and lead to a successful and accurate completion of the return for which you are legally responsible.

2.3 MINIMISING THE LIABILITY

Careful study of this chapter will indicate how in many cases an individual's tax liability can be reduced. This subject was discussed in Chapter 1, section 1.6, but is worth repetition. In particular consideration should be given to the following courses of action:

- Obtain all the possible reliefs and allowances.
- Take advantage of opportunities for tax-free investments, as discussed in Chapter 3, Investment Income.
- A married couple should ensure that no allowances are lost because one partner has insufficient taxable income. This could be achieved by, for example, transferring investments to the party with insufficient income, or ensuring that an adequate but defendable salary is paid to that party for services to a business carried out by the other partner. The transfer of investments may also be effective in reducing inheritance tax.
- One party's liability for higher rate tax may be reduced or eliminated by a transfer of income to the other party in the manner suggested above.
- From 6 April 2000, couples both under 65 on this date lost the married couples' allowance, but a claim to transfer the allowance between them still applies for 1999/00. This is because the whole or part of the married couple's allowance can be the allowance but the husband's income is not. The tax deduction in 1999/00 was £197 (£1 970 x 10%). Over 65 couples can still transfer the allowance for 2000/01.
- Where income is received from self-employment, part-time work or an unincorporated business owned by the taxpayer, ensure that all allowable expenses are charged in the business accounts.
- Where one party's potential capital gains are likely to exceed the annual threshold of £7 200 in 2000/01 (£7 100 in 1999/00). This would be another situation where a transfer of investments to the party with lower potential gains would be desirable. Since capital gains tax is payable at marginal income tax rates, such transfers would be particularly effective where the transferor is liable to tax at the higher rate, but the other party is not so liable.

2.4 SPECIMEN COMPUTATIONS

(a) 2000/01 – Married person paying basic rate tax only.

The following hypothetical example shows the various Schedules and cases under which the taxpayer was assessed:

		£
Schedule A, Net rental income		2 000
Schedule D, Case I. Profits as self-employed		4 000
Schedule D, Case III. Interest paid gross		100
Schedule D, Case IV. Interest on foreign bonds		200
Schedule D, Case VI. Net holiday lettings		1 000
Schedule E, Salary from employment		20 000
Statutory income		27 300
Less: charges on income		2 075
Total (net) income		25 225
Less: Allowances		
Personal	4 385	
		4 385
Chargeable income		20 840
Tax thereon		
£1 520 at 10%	152.00	
£19 320 at 23%	4 250.40	
		4 402.40
Less: Married couple's allowance is abolished for non-pensioner couples from 6 April 2000		nil
		£4 402.40

The tax would normally have been paid, or deducted from the income, under the following schedules and cases:

	£
Sch A, 22% of £2 000	440.00
Sch D, Case I 22% of £4 000	880.00
Sch D, Case III accounted for in coding	–
Sch D, Case IV 22% of £200	44.00
Sch D, Case VI 22% of £1 000	220.00
	1 584.00

Sch E, deducted under PAYE		
Salary	£20 000	
Sch D Case III income	100	
	20 100	
Less Charges	2 075	
	18 025	
Less Allowances - 4 385	4 385	
Chargeable	£13 640	
Tax thereon:		
£ 1 520 at 10%	152.00	
£12 120 at 22%	2 666.40	
£13 640		2818.40
		£4 402.40

(b) 1999/OO. Married person liable for higher-rate tax.
Assume that in this year the person receives a large bonus, so that total income becomes:

	£	£
Total income		44 385
Less: Allowances - Personal	4 385	
		4 385
Chargeable income		40 000

The chargeable income now exceeds the threshold of £28 400 at which higher rate is payable and the tax liability becomes:

		£
£ 1 520	at 10%	152.00
£26 880	at 22%	5 913.50
£28 400		6 065.60
£11 600	at 40%	4 640.00
£40 000		10 705.60
Less: Married couples allowance (now abolished)		nil
		£10 705.60

2.5 RELIEFS AND ALLOWANCES

(a) Personal allowance. This allowance applies to persons of either sex, whether married or not. Thus, under independent taxation both husband and wife obtain the allowance. The allowance depends on the age of the taxpayer and is as follows:

	1998/99	*1999/00*	*2000/01*
	£	*£*	*£*
Age below 65 years	4 195	4 335	4 385
65-74	5 410	5 720	5 790
75 and over	5 600	5 980	6 050

(b) Married couple's allowance, widow's bereavement allowance, and child allowance. From 6 April 2000, the allowances explained in this section were mostly abolished. Only a small part of one allowance remains. The married couple's allowance for pensioners remains for those who can claim it at 5 April 2000. A married pensioner who was 65 on 5th April 2000 can claim it, but one who became 65 on 6th April 2000 cannot. A single pensioner who was 65 before 6th April 2000 who later marries can claim the married couple's allowance.

(i) Married couple's allowance. (From 6 April 2000, pensioner couples only)

This allowance is given primarily to the husband but can be transferred to the wife, provided they are living together or he is responsible for her maintenance. A couple can choose to allocate the whole allowance to the wife, or she could claim, as of right, half the allowance. The tax relief on the allowance was restricted in 1999/00 to 10%. For subsequent years, please see opening paragraph above. A transfer would be an advantage where the husband could not use the allowance. The allowance is as follows:

	1998/99	*1999/00*	*2000/01*
	£	*£*	*£*
Age below 65 years	1 900	1 970	–
*Husband or wife 65-74	3 305	5 125	5 185
*Husband or wife 75 plus	3 345	5 195	5 255

*These allowances are reduced by half of the amount by which the taxpayer's income exceeds £16 800 in 1999/00 and £17 000 in 2000/01. The minimum allowance for 2000/01 is £2,000.

(ii) Widow's bereavement allowance

This allowance effectively means that in the tax year when the husband dies, and the following year, his widow obtained the equivalent of the married couple's allowance. From 1999/00, tax relief on the allowance was restricted to 10%. The allowance (before restriction) is £2 000 in 2000/01 and £1 970 in 1999/00. It is abolished for deaths after 5 April 2000. (There was no equivalent widower's allowance.)

(iii) Additional personal allowance for child (abolished 6 April 2000)

This allowance could be claimed by widows, widowers, single persons or by a married man whose wife was totally incapacitated. This allowance applied where the person had a child living with him or her and the child was under the age of sixteen at the beginning of the tax year; or was over that age and receiving full-time education or training or, if not the claimant's own child, was resident with and maintained by the claimant. From 6 April 1989, only one allowance was normally obtainable for a child. However, if a bedroom was kept available for the child to visit, and also some personal belongings were stored there, an allowance could be claimed. This was a common situation following a marriage breakdown. In 1999/00, tax relief on the allowance was restricted to 10%. The allowance (before restriction) was £1 900 in 1998/99 and £1 970 in 1999/00. It was abolished from 6 April 2000.

(c) Blind persons. If the taxpayer is registered as a blind person for the whole or part of a year an allowance of £1 400 in 2000/01 and £1 380 in 1999/00 may be claimed. Where the allowance is not needed, it can in certain circumstances be transferred to the taxpayer's husband or wife. The allowance is available for the year previous to the year of registration on proof of blindness at the end of that previous year (ESC. 6.10.94).

2.6 CHILDREN

Child benefits. These are cash payments payable to mothers from 4 April 1977 in respect of children under 19 years of age (Child Benefit Act 1975). They are exempt from tax (for the moment).

Where child benefits do not apply. Child benefits may not be payable in respect of children under 19 years of age living in certain overseas countries – for example, the former USSR, Asia, India, Pakistan, Africa and the Americas – where there are no reciprocal arrangements for social security benefits.

Scholarships. Income from a scholarship for full-time education is exempt from income tax so far as the holder of the scholarship is concerned. However, in the case of a scholarship paid for by the employer of a director or employee earning £8 500 p.a. or more, the cash value of a scholarship for a member of their family will normally be treated as part of their remuneration, subject to qualifications where payment is made from a trust fund.

Adopted children. By an extra-statutory concession in 1983 no tax will be charged on allowances paid to people who adopt children under government-approved schemes.

Child care. No tax is payable by an employee for the value of a place in a nursery provided by the employer for the employee's child. Tax is however payable by an employee on a cash allowance, voucher for child care or fees paid for child care if paid by the employer to the employee. Fees paid by the employer direct to nurseries, etc., and minders are taxable on directors and on employees earning £8 500 or more. The new Working Families Tax Credit (WFTC) from Autumn 1999 includes a child care tax credit. This credit will meet 70% of eligible childcare costs up to a maximum of £100 per week for one child families and £150 for families with 2 or more children. No tax relief is available to individuals for payments they make for child care.

2.7 HUSBAND AND WIFE

In most circumstances the following particular rules apply:

- Each party obtains a personal allowance – £4 385 in 2000/01 (£4 395 in 1999/00), increased for those aged 65 and over.
- Income from property owned jointly by husband and wife is assumed to be shared equally.

[Please see major changes proposed for 2000/01 in 2.5 above for all the following bullet points]

- The husband obtained, in addition, a married couple's allowance of £1 970 in 1999/00, also increased if husband or wife is aged 65 or over. The parties must be living together (or the husband be maintaining a separated wife) for this further allowance to apply. In the year of marriage, it is reduced by 1/12th for each month (beginning on the sixth of each month) before marriage.
- The whole or part of the allowance can be transferred to the wife.
- No transfer of excess allowances is available where the couple are separated, but where the husband is continuing to support the wife he will obtain the further allowance as above. This also applies in reverse.
- Additional personal allowance. Either party may claim this allowance or it may be apportioned between them by agreement. (See above.)
- Maintenance payments are made to a divorced or separated husband or wife who has not remarried, either for his or her maintenance or that of their children aged under 21, under a written agreement or Court Order. After 15 March 1988 tax relief for the payer was limited to the married couple's allowance (see above); and the payments will not be taxable in the recipient's hands. The payer obtains tax relief. From 1993 tax relief applies to payments made through the Child

Support Agency, but not directly to the child. From 6 April 1995 tax relief was at 15%, and for 1999/00 (only) at 10%. (See above.)

2.8 SALARIES, WAGES AND DIRECTORS' FEES

Introduction

For most people the greater part, if not the whole, of their income consists of the salary, wages, commission, bonuses and fees they draw under a contract of employment. This part of a taxpayer's income is assessed in accordance with the rules of Schedule E. The most important of these rules are considered in this section.

The majority of tax under Schedule E is collected by deduction from remuneration by means of the Pay As You Earn (PAYE) system, which is considered later. Remuneration is chargeable to tax in the tax year in which it is paid, even though the amount paid may refer to a previous tax year – see below.

The Cases under Schedule E

The question whether a taxpayer is resident or ordinarily resident in the UK decides the Case under which his income from employment is assessed. The vast majority of persons are assessed under Case I, which covers persons resident and ordinarily resident in the UK whose duties are wholly or mainly carried out in the UK. Case II covers remuneration for duties carried out in the UK for persons not resident or not ordinarily resident. Case III covers UK residents whose duties are carried out wholly abroad. The rules covering income from abroad are considered in Chapter 7, section 7.5.

The Pay As You Earn system (PAYE)

(a) General

The following notes are intended to indicate only the general nature and scope of the PAYE system. More detailed information is available from Tax Offices where a comprehensive pamphlet, the *Employer's Guide to PAYE,* can be obtained.

PAYE is the system under which employers are obliged to deduct income tax and National Insurance contributions from their employees' remuneration. The amount to be deducted is found from tax tables which take into account, by a coding system, the reliefs and allowances to which each employee is entitled. The employee's code is notified by the tax office to the employer and to the employee who, in addition, receives details showing how this particular code is made up. The employee should ensure that he or she is receiving all the applicable reliefs and allowances.

The remuneration from which the deductions are made includes all income from the employment, including salaries, wages, holiday pay, bonuses, fees, commission, pensions (to retired employees), most sickness benefits and some taxable benefits provided by the employer, the amount of which must be notified to the employee.

In order to assist self assessment employers have to issue their employees a P60 by 31 May of each year.

(b) Benefits

In the case of most benefits provided by the employer, such as the provision of a company car, the benefit will be outside the PAYE deduction scheme. In those cases the benefit will be taken into account in the code, so that the tax collected under PAYE will be increased by the necessary amount. Employers have to provide a copy of Form P11D to the employee by 6 July of each year.

(c) Deductions from pay

Where the remuneration is subject to deduction of the tax under PAYE, the amount to be taken into account is the amount before deductions, such as National Insurance Contributions (NIC) and allowable trade union subscriptions. However, where contributions to the employer's approved pension scheme are allowable, the amount of the contribution will reduce the amount of the pay on which PAYE is operated. Further payments subject to PAYE are redundancy pay where this is taxable, and certain advance payments of directors' fees.

An employee can arrange for contributions to approved charities to be deducted from remuneration and paid by the employer to specific charities, these contributions reducing pay for tax purposes.

(d) Refunds

When an employee has experienced a period of low remuneration, such as during sickness or unemployment, refunds may be due, but no refund can be made while an employee is involved in a trade dispute.

(e) Records

In addition to making correct deductions from employees' pay, an employer has to keep accurate records which may be inspected by tax officials, and submit annual returns; these returns include P11D forms showing the expenses and benefits of directors and employees receiving more than £8 500 p.a., and P9D forms showing expenses of other employees. An employer also has to provide employees with certificates of pay and tax deducted at the end of each tax year, and P45 forms with similar information when an employee leaves the employment.

(f) The codes

Apart from the issue of codes a tax office will not provide an employer with any information about an employee's affairs. The codes do, however, provide some information. Thus a code with the suffix H indicates that the taxpayer receives the married couple's allowance or the additional personal allowance; L indicates the personal allowance; codes P and V include the age allowance for single and married couples respectively. Where an employee does not wish this information disclosed he should apply for code T, which is used for special cases, such as where there is no 'free pay' (i.e. no allowances are given by the code OT) or, where no tax is deductible, code NT. The code BR indicates that the tax is deducted at the basic rate. The prefix D shows that higher rates are payable.

Code K

This applies where coding reductions exceed allowances. The coding reductions might cover occupational pensions, taxable benefits and untaxed income (e.g. on certain savings). Under the old code F the income in excess of the allowances was estimated and could only have the effect of reducing the allowances to nil. As a result the excess of the income over the allowances was subject to assessment at the end of the year. Under the K code such assessments should no longer be necessary as this new code deducts actual income (not estimated income) from the allowances, and if a surplus of income results that amount is added to pay or occupational pension.

Receipts basis of taxing remuneration

(a) General. From 6 April 1989 employees, including directors, have been taxed for a tax year on the remuneration actually received, or assumed to be received in that year. The new basis did not change the system for taxing regular payments of salaries and wages which were already taxed on a receipts basis and were subject to deductions for PAYE. It did, however, affect remuneration which is paid in a tax year after the year in which it is earned. This is often the case where directors' fees and bonuses are dependent on profits and cannot therefore be determined or paid until after the end of the accounting year of the business.

(b) Time of receipt of remuneration. It will be assumed that an individual has received remuneration at the earliest of the following times:

- When payment is made.
- When the employee or director becomes entitled to payment (which

may be after the accounting year in which the remuneration is earned).

- When remuneration is credited to an employee's or director's account with the paying company. This would be the situation with many directors, especially of smaller companies, where it is the practice to credit remuneration or fees of directors to their current account, and to pay part or all of the balance on that account when the cash position permits.
- Where, however, remuneration is determined during the course of an accounting year, it is assumed to be received at the end of that year.
- Where remuneration for an accounting period is determined after the end of that period, it will be taxed in the fiscal year when it is determined.
- Chargeable benefits are to be treated as received for tax purposes when the benefits are provided.

These rules apply to PAYE deductions.

(c) Earnings before 6 April 1989. Before this date it had been the general practice to assess directors' fees on the so-called 'accounts basis'. This meant that the fees included in the business accounts, whenever paid, were assessed for the fiscal year in which the accounting year ended. Thus if fees of, say, £50 000 were charged in the accounts drawn up to 31 December 1988, they would be assessed on the director for the tax year 1988/89.

(d) Treatment in business computation. Remuneration charged in the business accounts in a particular accounting year is, of course, normally an allowable deduction in computing profits under Schedule D for that year. However, if remuneration is paid nine months or more after the end of an accounting period ending after 5 April 1989 in which it is charged, that remuneration is not deductible in computing that year's taxable profit. It will be observed that where this rule applies the taxable profit for the year when the remuneration arises will be so much greater than the accounts profit.

If a tax calculation is made within the nine-month period, and the remuneration has not then been paid, that remuneration will be disallowed in the calculation, and allowed later when the remuneration is paid. However, the calculation can be adjusted if the remuneration is subsequently paid within the nine-month period; but a claim for this purpose must be made to the Inspector of Taxes within two years of the end of the accounts period concerned.

Compensation for loss of employment

If the compensation arises out of the contract of employment it is taxable in the hands of the recipient, unless paid for disability or injury, special contributions to approved retirement schemes, foreign service (with conditions) and terminal grants to members of the armed forces. By a statutory concession dated 2 September 1993 legal costs received as a result of pursuing a claim are not taxable. Voluntary payments made to an employee after his employment has ceased are exempt from tax up to £30 000 from 1988/89 onwards (but only where the Superannuation Funds Office has approved the pension scheme), and so are payments made under the Redundancy Payments Act 1965.

2.9 TAXABLE BENEFITS

General

Liability to tax under Schedule E may arise on benefits provided for an employee in addition to his salary, and these benefits may be in kind rather than cash. Particular examples of taxable benefits include the use of company cars, free accommodation, loans at beneficial rates, the provision of suits and television sets and free travel and credit card payments.

The general principle is that the cash equivalent of the benefits will be assessed under Schedule E on directors, and on employees earning £8 500 (including the value of the benefits). The rules do not apply to full-time working directors earning less than £8 500 who, with their relatives and associates (e.g. partners), own no more than 5% of the company's share capital. Employees earning less than £8 500 may be assessed on benefits received if such benefits are convertible into cash. The cash equivalent will in most cases be the cost to the employer, less any reimbursement by the employee.

From 1 December 1993 employers can no longer avoid paying National Insurance contributions or PAYE in respect of what the Budget of November 1993 described as 'exotic payments in kind'. Interest on loans to employees below a commercial rate will be taxable as a benefit.

The case of Pepper v. Hart, 1993, established that the cost of a benefit shall for tax purposes be based on the marginal, not average, cost. Marginal cost means essentially the additional cost to the employer for providing the benefit. It is likely that there will be problems in arriving at marginal cost and that some of these problems will be resolved by legislation or statements of Inland Revenue practice. Pepper v. Hart specifically concerned the benefit obtained by teachers who obtained places at reduced fees for their children in schools where the teachers were employed; in these cases the Inland Revenue has announced that no benefit will arise for payments of at least 15% of normal fees. Likewise it is accepted that the marginal cost of employees' travel in transport undertakings is nil where passengers paying normal fares are not displaced; and company goods sold to employees at not less than the wholesale price will not produce taxable benefits.

In the case of an asset placed at the disposal of a director, or employee earning more than £8 500, or members of their families, the cost is deemed to be the annual value of the benefit. The annual value of accommodation is the letting value.

From 5 April 1990 no tax has been charged on the benefit for higher paid employees on nursery facilities provided by employers.

Returns of benefits in kind for directors and higher-paid employees are made on form P11D, but for certain expenses a dispensation can be obtained from reporting on this form.

Business cars

(a) General. Taxpayers receive a benefit from the private use of business cars and this benefit is, in general, taxable; conversely, taxpayers can obtain tax allowances for the business use of their private cars. The treatment for tax purposes differs according to whether the taxpayer using the car is self-employed, an employee earning under £8 500 a year, a director or an employee earning £8 500 p.a. and above. The Inland Revenue is authorised to supply lists to the DSS of employers liable for Class 1A National Insurance contributions on these benefits.

(b) Employees (not directors) earning under £8 500 p.a. No taxable benefit is chargeable for the use of a car provided by the employer, provided some use of the car is made for business. However, the figure of £8 500 includes all the potentially taxable benefits.

(c) Self-employed persons. Capital allowances up to £3 000 p.a. may be obtained for vehicles used for business purposes, but these allowances will be reduced by the proportionate private mileage of the vehicle. Likewise the cost of fuel, maintenance, insurance and tax charged in the business accounts will need to be reduced for private use of the vehicle.

(d) Volunteer drivers. Volunteer drivers are liable for tax on any profit made on mileage allowances received from hospitals and similar volunteer organisations. The profit is the excess of the mileage allowances received over the Inland Revenue estimate of the cost per mile of running and maintaining the car.

(e) Company directors and employees earning £8 500 p.a. or more. The 1999 Budget announced major changes in the taxation of company car benefits. From 2002/2003, the charge will be based on carbon dioxide emissions. This will be applied on a percentage (max 35%) of the car's original price when new. For the years prior to this, the various discounts have been changed. From 6 April 1999 the taxable benefit arising from the use of company cars is calculated as 35% of the list price of cars when new. The charge is 25% of list price (23.45%

previously) for business mileage of 2 500 to 17 999 and 15% (11.55%) for mileage of 18 000 miles or more. A further reduction of one quarter (previously one third) applies to cars four or more years old at the end of the tax year. In addition fuel scale charges are applied as scheduled below.

Disabled drivers

The cost of converting a company car for use by a disabled person is no longer included in the price of the car for car benefit purposes.

Cars fuel scale charges

	1999/00		*2000/01*	
	Petrol	*Diesel*	*Petrol*	*Diesel*
Engine size cc	*£*	*£*	*£*	*£*
0–1400	1 210	1 540	1 700	2 170
1401–2000	1 540	1 540	2 170	2 170
2001 +	2 270	2 270	3 200	3 200

Vans under 3.5 tonnes. From 6 April 1993 a standard charge of £500 is taxable where a van is provided by an employer for the private use of an employee. For vans four years old at the end of the tax year the benefit is reduced to £350. The benefit is reduced proportionately for vans incapable of being used for 30 days in a year. A van can be a car converted to carry goods or tools, etc. This would be by the removal of the rear seats, seat belts, etc. It has to be incapable of being reconverted in less than an 'evening'.

Company cars sold to employees. The employee may be liable for tax on the excess of the market value over the price at which the car is sold to him. This particularly applies to cars previously leased to customers.

Employees' cars – General rules. If an employee is necessarily obliged to use his own car on his employer's business, the employee can deduct the expenses of doing so from any reimbursement he receives from the employer. The reimbursement normally takes the form of a mileage rate. Any surplus which results is taxable in the employee's hands and a deficiency is a tax-allowable deduction from the employee's earnings. It is interesting to note that these rules also apply to the use of the employee's horse and now (from 6 April 1999) bicycle at 12p per mile! It is, however, necessary to record and justify records of business and private mileage and of the expenses incurred, the expenses being apportioned on the basis of the proportionate business mileage. Obviously difficulties arise in keeping accurate records and for this reason the Fixed Profit Car Scheme, explained below, is easier to operate.

Cash alternative. When the use of a company car was readily convertible into cash by the employee (i.e. a director and those earning £8 500 a year or more) the cash equivalent was chargeable to tax in the employee's hands. The employer is liable to pay Class 1A National Insurance contributions on the benefit (TA 1988 S.19). If the employee receives a higher salary instead of the use of a company car that employee will, in the normal course, be liable to tax on the higher salary. Even in the case where an option to take a higher salary is offered by the employer, the employee will pay tax on the option of the higher salary (Heaton v Bell 1969).

Fixed Profit Car Scheme (FPCS). Under this scheme employees may claim tax-free mileage allowances for business use of their own cars, according to the scale shown below.

The 'tax-free' FPCS rates which apply for business mileage are the same for 1997/98 to 2000/01, and are as follows:

	on the first 4 000 miles in the tax year	on each mile over 4 000 miles in the tax year
Size of car engine		
up to 1 000 cc	28p	17p
1 000 - 1 500 cc	35p	20p
1 500 - 2 000 cc	45p	25p
over 2 000 cc	63p	36p

If the employee receives from the employer a mileage rate greater than the sum above, the employee will be taxed on the excess. This problem is likely to arise when mileage above 4000 miles is reimbursed at the rate applicable to mileage below that figure. Any deficit between the amount received and the above rates or actual costs incurred can be claimed against tax. Relief for interest is *not* included in FPCS rates and needs to be claimed for separately.

Gifts, gratuities and parties

In general, gifts are taxable in the hands of employees if they arise out of the employment. Typical examples of taxable gifts are tips, footballers' benefits and Christmas gifts. Gift vouchers are assessable at their cost to the employer, but luncheon vouchers for no more than 15p a day are not assessable; nor are meals in a canteen available for employees generally or long-service awards to employees up to £20 per year of service. Gifts to employees by third parties are not taxable up to £150 (to 5 April 1996 £100) p.a., nor is entertainment provided by third parties. Modest expenditure on staff parties, e.g. at Christmas, is not regarded as a benefit if less than £75 per person. The expenditure, from 6 April 1995, may be spent on more than one event as long as the total is not exceeded. If one function costs more than £75 per head the whole amount is assessed. If more than £75 is spent one more than one event or function it is those functions which take the expenditure over £75 and beyond which are assessable.

Gift aid

Charitable gifts by individuals and close companies qualify for tax relief. From 6 April 2000, there is no longer a minimum (previously a minimum of £250 net of basic rate tax).

From 6 April 2000, the upper limit on gifts deducted from wages is abolished (previously a maximum of £1 200 p.a.)The Government will pay a 10% supplement on payroll giving donations for 3 years from April 2000.

Accommodation

Where an employee is provided with a house or other accommodation rent free or at a rent below the gross rateable annual value, he or she will normally be liable to pay tax on the annual value, reduced by the rent the employee pays. This does not apply to employees such as caretakers who are required to live in the accommodation as part of their duties, but the only directors who can obtain the advantage of this exemption are full-time working directors, or directors of non-profit-making companies, and they must have no material interest in the company. Accommodation provided for directors where there is a threat to their security is also exempt. The cost of heating, lighting, cleaning, repairs (other than structural repairs), maintenance, decoration, furniture and domestic effects, which is not met by the employee, must not exceed 10% of his or her emoluments.

Where an employee first occupies the house provided by his or her employers on and after 31 March 1983, and the cost of providing the accommodation exceeds £75 000, the employee may be liable for tax at the official rate of interest on the excess. From 6 April 1996 this additional charge was removed. Where the property has been held for six years before the employee's occupation the cost becomes the market value with vacant possession.

In 1990/91 and onwards companies cannot reclaim VAT on the provision of free accommodation for directors or their families.

Relocation: employees moving house

From 5 April 1993 an employer may make a tax-free contribution of up to £8 000 for removal expenses of employees; the relief applies even if the employee retains the existing house, such as for letting. Relief for additional housing costs is withdrawn. The payments are not subject to PAYE but those over £8 000 must be recorded by the employer on forms P9D or P11D (FA 1993 S 76 and Sch 5).

Business expenses

In the case of directors, and employees earning more than £8 500, the expenses or expense allowances paid by the business are assessable on the individual. It is then necessary for the employee or director to satisfy the Inspector of Taxes that the expenses were incurred for the purpose of the business.

From 6 April 1995 tax relief applies to certain incidental personal expenses paid by employers in respect of employees who are obliged to stay away from their homes overnight for business purposes. The most common such expenses include newspapers, telephone charges and laundry. The allowable amounts are £5 a night in the UK and £10 a night overseas. Payments above these limits are wholly chargeable to tax.

Beneficial loans

Where a loan is made by a business to an employee earning above £8 500, or a director, the individual will be chargeable to tax on the annual amount of interest below an 'official rate' to be notified by statutory instrument.

In 1994/95 and onwards, tax exemption applies where an employee's cheap or interest-free loans total no more than £5 000. This excludes cheap loans which qualify for tax relief, such as mortgages. For mortgages the taxpayer will pay tax at his marginal rate on the benefit of a cheap loan but will obtain tax relief on the commercial rate of interest under the MIRAS rules.

By concession an employee is not chargeable with tax on the benefit of cheap interest on a 'bridging loan' from his or her employer obtained because he or she had to change his residence owing to being transferred in the organisation. This concession applies to a loan outstanding for up to 12 months and not exceeding £30 000.

Income tax is not payable by employees on loans from employers whose business includes the lending of money, provided the loan is made on the same terms as are available to the public, ignoring differences in initial fees of administration (FA 1994).

Medical insurance

The cost of medical insurance provided by an employer is assessable on directors and employees earning above £8 500 . From 1982/83 this benefit is not taxable for employees earning under £8 500 p.a., and is in no case taxable for work overseas.

From 2 July 1997 new contracts for medical insurance for people aged 60 or over are not eligible for tax relief.

Statutory Maternity Pay (SMP)

Under the Employee Protection Act 1975 maternity pay can be paid to an employee after the employee ceases to work due to pregnancy. These payments are taxable under Schedule E if the contract of employment still exists, and tax is deducted under Schedule E. If the contract of employment has been terminated at the time of payment, tax is chargeable under Schedule D Case VI, and the payments may be made gross.

Season tickets

From 1982/83 the value of season tickets for travel to work provided by employers for employees is assessable on the employees, but loans made by employers for employees to buy season tickets are generally exempt.

Credit cards

From 1982/83 the value of purchases under credit cards made payable and chargeable to employers is taxable in the hands of the employees.

Armed Forces leave travel

Warrants or allowances for leave travel by members of the armed forces are exempt from tax.

2.10 LIABILITY INSURANCE AND UNINSURED LIABILITIES

On and after 6 April 1995 liability insurance on work-related risks is tax-free for employees and gives tax relief when paid for by employers. The tax-free relief applies for 6 years after the end of the employment. Also tax-free are payments for uninsured work-related charges which could have been insured, and these charges could include legal costs in defending an action.

2.11 LIFE ASSURANCE

To 13 March 1984. Policies made up to this date, and not subsequently amended, provide relief from income tax by means of a deduction of 12.5% from 6 April 1989 (previously 15%) from the premium payments. For the purpose of this relief the premiums could not exceed the greater of one sixth of the taxpayer's net income after charges, or £1 500 in a tax year.

After 13 March 1984. The above relief is withdrawn for policies taken out after this date and for existing policies where the benefits are subsequently improved.

2.12 NATIONAL INSURANCE AND SOCIAL SECURITY

Details of the current National Insurance contributions and benefits are obtainable from various pamphlets issued by the Department of Social Security. Contributions are divided into four classes, as follows:

Class 1. Employed persons.
Class 2. Self-employed persons.
Class 3. Voluntary contributions.
Class 4. Earnings-related contributions payable by the self-employed on earnings above a minimum, in addition to Class 2 contributions.

The contributions do not give relief from income tax. Employers' contributions under Class 1 are, however, deductible charges in computing taxable profits. Class 1a contributions are made by employers who provide private cars for use by directors and higher-paid employers. Major changes to Class 2 and Class 4 contributions come into force from April 2000. This is to remove the benefits of self-employment compared to normal employment.

Social security benefits

(a) Taxable. Retirement pension, widow's pensions and allowances; statutory sick pay (see below); statutory maternity pay; guardians and special allowances for children. The Job Seekers Allowance, excepting the earnings-related supplement and benefits to strikers' families, is taxable from 5 July 1982. There are a number of qualifications.

(b) Not taxable. Child benefit, benefits for sickness benefit (but not statutory sick pay), maternity, invalidity, incapacity, industrial injury; mobility allowance; death grant; income support; housing credit; attendance allowance; family credit; supplementary benefits and pensions for wounds or disability payable to members of the armed forces, merchant seamen, and to civilians for war injury; war widows' pensions; and child dependency allowances. The Job Finder's grant is tax-free.

(c) Statutory sick pay (SSP). This is a payment which an employer is bound to make to most employees for absence due to sickness from 3 to up to 28 weeks in a tax year. It is recoverable by the employer plus 7.5% for administration, by deduction from payments of National Insurance contributions, with a National Insurance bill of under £20 000. Larger companies will not receive reimbursement. It forms part of the employee's income for tax and National Insurance purposes.

Self certificates only are required for NI purposes for 4-7 days' sickness, and doctors' certificates for longer periods.

Married women paying reduced rates of NI contributions are entitled to SSP.

The following are not entitled to SSP:

- Where other state benefits have been received.
- Where the maximum entitlement of SSP has been received.
- Those on strike.

In addition to the statutory entitlement to SSP an employee may be entitled to what is called 'occupational sick pay' (OSP) from the employer under his or her contract of service or custom in the employment. The rules of OSP may involve a deduction for SSP and state sickness benefits. Payments of OSP are also taxable in the employee's hands, except to the extent that the employee has contributed to a fund for the purpose.

The detailed rules for the calculation and eligibility for SSP can be complicated in particular cases and further information can be obtained from the Department of Social Security.

(d) Unemployment and strikes – Job Seeker's Allowance (JSA). The Job Seeker's Allowance, received by the unemployed person and one adult dependant (e.g. wife, husband, parent), is taxable and forms part of the taxpayer's total income for tax purposes in a tax year. Additions for children are not taxable.

Where the unemployment is prolonged, and the total income including JSA is consequently small, a refund of tax already paid (e.g. under PAYE) may be due. This would apply if the total income in a tax year to 5 April was below the personal and other allowances to which the taxpayer was entitled. This refund could not be obtained while benefit was being paid but would be paid soon after the next 5 April or, possibly, if the taxpayer obtained employment before that date.

As no tax is deducted from the benefits, and if the taxpayer's other income is sufficiently high, he or she might be liable for unpaid tax at the end of the tax year. This unpaid amount would be collected in the following tax year, usually by adjustment to the PAYE code if the taxpayer was then in employment.

Long-term unemployment means persons who have been out of work for at least two years. When unemployed persons obtain employment the following provisions apply from 6 April 1995: employers obtain a full rebate of National Insurance contributions for 1 year; for *all* employees earning less than £205 a week employer National Insurance contributions are reduced by 0.6%; from 6 April 1996 the employers' NIC holiday includes trainees; 3-week work trial places are available for persons who have been unemployed for over 6 months and who will continue to receive their benefits; the Job Finders' grant is available for those who have been unemployed for over 2 years and who take a lower-paid job. From 6 April 1995 this is free from tax.

Supplementary benefit for persons who do not have to make themselves available for employment is not taxable. Such persons include those over retirement age, single parents of children under 16, and those looking after disabled people.

Persons on strike. No benefit is payable to persons on strike, but supplementary benefit may be payable to a wife and this benefit is taxable. Tax is not deducted from the benefit. If any refund of tax is due it cannot be paid until the taxpayer returns to work, and if there is additional tax payable it will be recovered by adjustment to the taxpayer's PAYE coding for a future year. In all cases the tax payable for a tax year will be assessed soon after 5 April at the year end.

2.13 COVENANTS

General

A covenant is a 'settlement' in the form of a deed whereby one person undertakes to pay an annual or more frequent amount to another person or association. Although many are quite simple in form they often need professional drafting and advice. They are widely used for contributions to charities and for this purpose have tax benefits, provided they are expressed to be payable for over three years and are paid out of income, not capital. They were also widely used to support relatives and children, particularly students, but the tax benefits for covenants other than those for registered charities were abolished for covenants made after 15 March 1988.

Since charitable covenants must be paid out of income to obtain tax relief they are inappropriate for persons without taxable income, such as many married women. Joint covenants made by, for instance, husband and wife are assumed to be shared equally, so that the party without taxable income should withdraw from such a covenant.

Gross covenants

A gross covenant is where the agreed payment is a gross amount from which tax at the basic rate (where applicable) is deducted. Thus if A agrees to pay B £1 000 p.a. less tax, B would receive in 2000/01 £780 (because basic rate is 22%). Subject to the following qualifications B (if not liable for tax) could then recover from the Inland Revenue the tax deducted, making the payment worth the gross amount of £1 000 in B's hands. This system applies only to covenants for registered charities. A's income for tax purposes would be reduced by £1 000 for calculating his or her higher rate, and he or she would recover the basic rate by deduction from the payment.

Net covenants

A net covenant is one where the covenanter undertakes to pay a regular net amount which is fixed and does not change with alterations in the basic rate of tax. If A had agreed to pay B a fixed annual amount of, say, £750 in 1995/96 this would represent a gross payment of £1 000 from which tax of £250 (25%) had been deducted. In 1996/97 the £750 actually paid represented a gross amount of £987, from which tax of £237 at 24% had been deducted. In 1997/98 this fell to £974 and £224 at the basic rate of 23%. In 2000/01, this falls to £961 and £211. The refund of tax due to B, if applicable, would thus have fallen from £250 to £211, and the set-off against A's taxable income would have fallen from £1 000 to £961. For these reasons, net covenants are to be avoided where there are prospects of a fall in the basic rate of tax. This is likely to have a significant effect upon charities' income. With the advent of limitless Gift Aid, covenants (apart from a regular giving habit) are replaces. (See above.)

2.14 INTEREST PAID AND HOME LOANS

Summary

In general interest payable by an individual on a debt or a loan, including hire purchase and overdraft interest, is not an allowable charge against his or her income for tax purposes. However, interest paid does give tax relief in the following cases: loans for the purchase of homes up to 5 April 2000; loans for business purposes; purchase of retirement annuities where the loan is charged on property; and letting of residential accommodation. These cases are considered briefly below.

Home loans - the following is of historical interest to 5 April 2000

- **General.** Interest payable to a 'qualified lender' on a loan up to £30 000 was an allowable charge (until 5 April 2000) against income where the loan is for the purchase of the principal private residence of the borrower. From 6 April 2000 this relief is abolished. The home must be in the UK or Ireland and may be a large caravan or houseboat. Qualified lenders include building societies, banks, insurance companies, local authorities and some friendly societies.
- **The tax relief.** By arrangement with the lender, and agreement of the Inland Revenue, in most cases the borrower paid the interest element of his or her repayments (not the capital element) subject to a deduction of 10% to 5 April 2000. However, the deduction of tax at 25% will remain for those over 65 who borrow to obtain a life annuity and whose loan was in existence at 9 March 1999 or subject to a written offer from a tender. The system of deducting tax at the basic rate is called MIRAS, or Mortgage Interest Relief At Source. Where a

borrower is not liable for tax the amount deducted can be retained.

- **Home improvement.** Interest on loans made by 5 April 1984 for the improvement of homes was allowable within the limit of £30 000, but this relief was abolished for such loans made after that date.
- **Dependent relatives.** The income tax relief applies to interest, within the limit, on loans to purchase homes for dependent relatives, e.g. mother and father, where the homes were bought and occupied by 5 April 1988. This relief was abolished, however, together with capital gains relief, for loans made or homes occupied after that date.
- **Unmarried couples.** From 1 August 1988, only one amount of relief for loans up to £30 000 applies to mortgage interest relief on a home. On loans taken out before that date each person sharing a home could obtain the maximum relief on the interest each pays. For interest on loans taken out after that date each sharer is entitled to claim an equal share of the £30 000 limit, i.e. for two sharers £15 000 each and for three sharers £10 000 each; the actual amount of relief is, of course, also limited to the actual interest each person pays. This may mean that the interest paid by one sharer is less than his or her proportionate share of the £30 000 limit. In this case the shortfall can be transferred to another sharer whose interest paid exceeds his or her proportionate share of the total limit, but not to the extent that the £30 000 limit is exceeded for the home.
- **Husbands and wives.** The basic principle is that tax relief on home loan interest is given to the party taking out the loan. Before independent taxation of women on 5 April 1990 husband and wife with a joint mortgage could have the tax relief allocated between them in any way they pleased or, strictly, according to the interest each paid. With a joint loan after 5 April 1990 the tax relief would normally be split equally between the two parties. However, an application can be made, within 12 months of the end of the year of assessment concerned, for the relief to be shared in other proportions. The relief would, of course, only apply to interest on up to £30 000 of the loan. With a loan subject to MIRAS (see above) relief from lower-rate tax is obtained by deduction from the interest element of the repayments.

  In the case of a non-MIRAS mortgage where one party was not liable for tax, an election should ensure that the taxpaying spouse received the maximum relief.

  The remaining situation where a reduction in the combined taxation of husband and wife could be obtained was where one spouse was over 65 and whose age allowance was restricted by having income above the limit. That person could reduce his or her income by receiving the appropriate share of the mortgage interest tax relief. Loan interest along with health insurance can no longer be used to reduce income for this limit. However, interest from TESSAs is not included.

- **Bridging loans.** These are loans obtained to buy a new home pending sale of the old one. Tax relief on the interest, within the limit, is obtainable for normally up to a year, with possible extension by agreement of the Inspector of Taxes.
- **Living away from home.** The relief is available for interest on a loan for the purchase of a house intended as the taxpayer's eventual home when the terms of employment require him or her to live elsewhere. This provision applies, for example, to vicars and to many tenants and managers of licensed premises; it also applies to the self-employed who are required under contract to live in job-related accommodation.
- **Sale of home.** When a home owner moves out of his or her principal private residence on which there is an outstanding mortgage tax relief continues to apply to the interest payable on or after 16 March 1993. This is provided that the house is offered for sale, and tax relief continues for up to 12 months after moving, with a possible extension at the discretion of the Inland Revenue in case of difficulty in selling the house. It is irrelevant whether the borrower buys a new house or moves to rented accommodation.

  On the sale of the old house the outstanding loan will normally be repaid but this may not be altogether possible where there is 'negative equity', i.e. the outstanding loan exceeds the proceeds on the sale of the house. In that case it may be possible to transfer the existing loan to be secured on the purchase of a new house with, if necessary, an additional advance to buy the latter. For tax relief the then total borrowing must not exceed the limit of £30 000.
- **Income support.** From October 1995 income support (such as for the unemployed) was reduced for existing mortgages and will not be payable for 9 months for persons taking out new mortgages.

Loans for business

Interest paid is an allowable expense where the loan is used for business purposes, including the interest on hire purchase transactions. Interest is also allowable in the following special cases:

- Loans for buying shares in partnership or loans to the partnership; this also applies to co-operatives. Since March 1981 the borrower need not be an active member of the partnership.
- Loans for acquiring ordinary shares in close companies or for loans to close companies (not investment companies). A close company is one controlled by five or less 'participators', meaning generally shareholders. The participator, his or her relatives and associates (e.g. partners), count as one person for this purpose. To qualify the borrower must either (i) own more than 5% of the ordinary shares in the company, or (ii) own some shares and work full-time in the company.

- Loans for enabling employees to acquire ordinary shares in an employee-controlled company. The employee or his or her spouse must work full-time in the company. The company must be resident in the UK, must be a trading company and 'unquoted', i.e. there is no quotation for its shares on a Stock Exchange, and 75% of its ordinary shares, and the voting power, must be in the hands of the employees or their spouses. Other conditions apply.

The relief is withdrawn where the entity of the borrower changes, except where the loan could have been treated as a new loan to the new business entity.

Loans to buy retirement annuities

Relief applies to the interest on a loan up to £30 000 secured on land or buildings.

Loans for let property

Relief on the interest is available provided that the property is let for at least 26 weeks in a year at a commercial rent.

Loans to directors and higher-paid employees

Where directors and employees earning over £8 500 a year receive loans from their employers at interest below a commercial rate the saving in interest is treated as a benefit and taxable under Schedule E.

By concession an employee is not chargeable with tax on the benefit of cheap interest on a 'bridging loan' from the employer obtained because he or she had to change residence owing to being transferred in the organisation. This concession applies to a loan outstanding for up to 12 months and not exceeding £30 000.

2.15 PROVIDING FOR RETIREMENT

General

Provisions for retirement fall under the following: (a) National Insurance retirement pensions; (b) occupational pensions operated by employers; (c) additional voluntary contributions (AVC) which supplement an employer's scheme; and (d) personal pension plans (PPP). The legislation is complex, particularly so far as (b), (c) and (d) are concerned, but the essentials are set out below.

National Insurance retirement pensions

The various classes of contribution were referred to in section 2.12 above. Full information as to the current contributions and the pension entitlements in various individual circumstances can be obtained from pamphlets issued by the Department of Social Security. No tax relief is given on contributions. Employers' contributions are tax-allowable deductions in computing business profits. The retirement pension forms part of the pensioner's total income for tax purposes; i.e. it is taxable, assuming the recipient is liable for tax. Basic rate tax is not, however, deducted from the pension because many retired people are not liable for tax.

A National Insurance pension paid to a wife forms part of her taxable income even though it was derived from her husband's contributions.

Employer's occupational pension schemes

These are pension schemes set up by employers for the benefit of their employees and are administered by trustees including employee representatives. Contributions to the fund are usually made by both employer and employee but in some cases only by the employer. In order that the tax benefits shall be obtained the schemes must conform to certain conditions and be approved by the Occupational Pensions Board.

Subject to these conditions the income of the fund is tax-free, the employer's contributions are allowable expenses in computing business profits, and the employee's contributions are deducted from remuneration before calculating his or her tax. The pension payable is taxable as earned income and tax is normally deducted from the payment according to the pensioner's code number.

For the tax benefits to be obtained, the pension must be no more than two thirds of final salary with a maximum of £91 000 on 6 April 2000 (£90 600 on 6 April 1999). These limits apply to new schemes established after 14 March 1989, and to employees entering existing schemes after 1 June 1989. However, pensions and lump sums in excess of these limits can be paid, for practical purposes involving separate funds, but the income of the separate funds and the contributions to them will not be eligible for tax relief. The schemes can provide for employees to retire at age 50 but 20 years' membership of the scheme is necessary for full relief. On leaving an employment contributions are returnable to an employee with less than two years' membership of the scheme.

Pensions can provide for increases in the cost of living even though such increases take the pension above two thirds of the salary limit. Pensions to people who retire early because of ill health can be based on the length of service which could otherwise have been complete (PR. 22.12.93 and FA 1987 and 1989).

The 1986 Finance Act provided that surpluses in occupational pension funds must be eliminated where such surpluses exceed 5% of liabilities. Refunds of such surpluses to employers attract tax at 40%. These provisions are designed to prevent the accumulation in pension funds of surpluses which have benefited from tax relief, and the tax-free distribution of such surpluses.

Additional voluntary contributions (AVC)

From October 1987 additional voluntary contributions to increase pensions (but not lump sums) may be paid by employees, either to the employer's pension scheme or to a 'free-standing' scheme of the employee's choice. Contributions may be made up to 15% of earnings (less payments to the employer's main scheme), subject to limits where earnings exceed £91 800 on 6 April 2000 (£90 600 on 6 April 1999). These additional contributions have the same tax benefits as for the main occupational pension scheme. The excess provided by the AVC will be refunded to the employee at retirement subject to tax at 10% above the employee's top rate, i.e. at 20% 32% or 50%, depending on total income. Where the contributions do not exceed £2 400 a year in a free-standing scheme the employer need not be involved in an AVC.

Personal pension plans (PPP)

(a) General nature of PPPs. These are schemes which, from 1 July 1988, were established by individuals to provide pensions and lump sum benefits with important tax reliefs. The legislation, now contained in Chapter III of the Taxes Act 1988 (as amended by the Finance Act 1989), applies to all new personal pension schemes although, of course, existing retirement annuity contracts remain valid. Personal pensions can be arranged with bodies authorised under the Financial Services Act 1986, including insurance companies, banks, building societies, unit trusts, etc., and individuals may have freedom to manage the investment of their contributions. The schemes must have Inland Revenue approval and are subject to many conditions of which the essentials are outlined below.

(b) The contributors. Personal pension plans are particularly suitable for the self-employed and are also applicable to employees not covered by a company occupational pension scheme, those who do not join such a scheme, and those in a company scheme who contract out of the State Earnings Related Pension Scheme (SERPS). Employers who do not operate company schemes, such as many small businesses, can contribute to the PPPs of their employees.

(c) The benefits. The schemes may provide for both annuities and lump sums on retirement, and provision can be made for spouses and dependants. The benefits can be paid when the subscriber is aged 50 to 75, but may be paid earlier than 50 in the case of infirmity or where customary in the occupation. They may be arranged for up to a fixed term of 10 years even if the subscriber dies within that period. The lump sum must be paid when the pension becomes due, and is limited to 25% of the accumulated benefits with a maximum of £150 000 (1989/90 and onwards). The actual benefits will be calculated on what is called 'money purchase' of the fund, i.e. what the scheme will buy at maturity.

An annuity may be deferred until the annuitant reaches age 75, but amounts roughly comparable with the annuity may be withdrawn. Deferral of an annuity may be appropriate in times when annuity rates are low. The annuity can be provided by both UK insurers and by those in the European Union.

(d) The contribution limits. The contribution limits eligible for tax relief for all of an individual's personal pensions are the following percentages of 'net relevant earnings' (effectively total earned income less allowable charges and expenses):

up to age 35	17.5%
age 36 to 45	20.0%
age 46 to 50	25.0%
age 51 to 55	30.0%
age 56 to 60	35.0%
61 and over	40.0%

The percentage limit for the lump sum is 5% of earnings. Any shortfall of contributions on these limits can be set back against the earnings of the previous year or can be carried forward for six years. It would be beneficial to carry back the contributions for a year in which tax rates were higher than when they were paid. The maximum earnings are £91 800 in 2000/01 and £90 600 in 1999/00.

(e) Tax reliefs. Within the limits indicated above the contributions give relief of tax to the subscriber, basic rate income tax being deducted from the payments. The income from the invested fund is free of income tax and capital gains tax. A lump sum paid out of the value of the fund on maturity is free of income tax and inheritance tax. The value of the fund on maturity may be converted into an annuity from an insurance company, and the consequent yearly payments of the annuity form part of the earned income of the annuitant and are taxable. The lump sum is calculated after providing for dependants' benefits.

(f) Assignment. Although a personal pension plan can include provision for dependants, the benefits cannot be assigned. The exception is where the accumulated fund is converted into an annuity for a fixed term and in this case the payments of the annuity after the death of the subscriber can be bequeathed by will.

Because of the tax reliefs, personal pension plans should represent good long-term investments. As means of providing for retirement they are particularly desirable for the self-employed and others not adequately covered by occupational pension schemes.

However, because contributions to occupational pension schemes are normally paid by employers, as well as employees, such schemes are often more beneficial.

2.16 VOCATIONAL TRAINING RELIEF (VTR)

Since April 1992 persons (including non-taxpayers) can obtain tax relief on the fees they pay for vocational training up to level 5 of the National Vocational Qualifications (NVQs). The relief is only available to UK residents who are not receiving assistance under government schemes for employment training, or student grants; and it applies to fees for study and examination, not to books or equipment. It does not apply to children under 16 years of age, nor to those aged 16 to 18 in full-time education at a school. A form must be completed to confirm eligibility for the relief, which is obtained by the trainee by deducting tax from the fees payable. The amount so deducted is reclaimed by the training organisation from the Inland Revenue. Application for higher-rate relief, where applicable, is made to the appropriate tax office. Inland Revenue leaflet 119 applies. (See PR 30.11.93 and 13.12.93.)

From 6 May 1996 relief is also allowable to persons aged over 30 who pay for their own retraining for new careers. VTR would apply whether or not the training course leads to a NVQ or Scottish equivalent. The VTR will be for full-time vocational courses lasting between four weeks and a year. Courses such as MBAs will for the first time fall within the scope of VTR.

2.17 DISABILITY INSURANCE

An individual is exempt from tax on the first 12 months of benefits from an insurance policy for which he or she pays and which provides benefits for loss of earnings due to sickness or disability.

CHAPTER 3

INVESTMENT INCOME

3.1 A SUMMARY OF THE SYSTEM

General

Investment income forms part of a taxpayer's income for tax purposes. However, much of it is taxed at source. Where this is so, the taxpayer has no more basic or lower rate tax to pay, but may be liable for the higher rate of 40% on the income. A taxpayer liable at only the lower rate can reclaim any excess deducted. The 1999 Budget announced that from 6 April 1999, a taxpayer whose marginal rate is the new 10% rate cannot reclaim tax suffered at 20%. During the passage of the 1999 Finance Act, this was reversed. Tax suffered on investment income at 20% can be reclaimed, if appropriate, from 6 April 1999. Investment income is called 'unearned income' and includes dividends and interest received. Earned income is that derived from the personal efforts of the taxpayer, such as salaries, fees and profits from unincorporated businesses. Investment income may be generally classified for tax purposes as: taxed interest, untaxed interest and taxed dividends. From 6 April 1999, dividends have been paid with a tax credit of 10%. This also applies to almost all other forms of investment income, including interest received from banks, building societies and unit trusts, from which 20% has been deducted. *No* further tax will be payable if the tax payer's top rate is 20% or the basic rate (22% in 2000/01). Only if the top rate is 40%, will tax on the top slice be due.

Taxed interest

Subject to the exceptions indicated below, interest received by the taxpayer is normally a net amount after the payer has deducted tax at the 20% rate. It includes interest received on company debentures, most government securities, local authority loans, other loans and deposits in building societies and banks. The taxpayer must enter the gross amount before tax on the return of income and it is the gross amount which forms part of the total income for the purpose, for example, of calculating any liability to higher-rate tax. From 6 April 1999, if the taxpayer's top rate of tax is the 10% band and they have suffered tax at 20% on interest received, they can now recover the excess – the previous restriction has ben reversed.

Untaxed interest

This refers to interest received without deduction of tax and would include interest from National Savings, government stock on the National Savings and Trustee Savings Bank registers, and 3½% War Loan. Tax is payable by assessment on untaxed interest, but it is particularly suitable for those not liable to tax, including charities. Individuals who are not liable for income tax can apply for interest to be paid gross. From 6 April 1996 tax on these sources is only liable at 20% if any tax is due.

Taxed dividends

(a) General. In the case of dividends, i.e. shares of profit received from limited companies, the situation is similar to that of taxed interest; the lower rate is said to be 'imputed' to the dividend. Up to 5 April 1999 this meant that the person receiving the dividend was assumed to have suffered tax at 20%. Higher-rate taxpayers would be liable for tax at 40% on the grossed-up dividend, less the tax credit of 20%, i.e. a net payment of 20%. If an individual's total tax liability was less than the tax imputed to dividend income, and deducted from taxed interest, etc., the excess could be reclaimed.

From 1999/00 the tax credit on dividends was reduced to 10%, but *cannot* be reclaimed if the individual's total tax liability is less than the tax imputed. The 10% tax credit will continue to satisfy the tax liability at lower and basic rates. Higher rate taxpayers will have an effective rate of 32.5%. This is to avoid a liability greater than that under the previous system, as illustrated by the following example:

	To 5 April 1999	From 6 April 1999
	£	£
UK dividend	80.00	80.00
Tax credit	20.00 (20% of gross)	8.89 (10% of gross)
Income	100.00	88.89
Higher tax rate	40.00 (40%)	28.89 (32.5%)
After-tax income	60.00	60.00

(b) Charities. Charities are normally exempt from tax and can as a result reclaim the tax imputed to dividends received from UK companies.

Dividends and interest from overseas

The tax deducted or imputed may include overseas tax as well as the UK basic rate. The latter deduction may be lower as a result of double taxation relief.

Accrued interest

From 28 February 1986 investment income for tax purposes includes accrued interest added to the price on the sale of certain securities. This would be the situation where the buyer would subsequently receive a payment of interest which covered the period before the purchase. On the other hand, if the sale was made close to the date when interest was payable, the seller would receive the interest and the proportion due to the buyer would be deducted from the price. Accrued interest is chargeable to tax only where the total nominal value of the securities owned by the taxpayer is above £5 000. The securities concerned are interest-bearing securities and stock, such as government securities, local authority loans and company debentures.

Likewise manufactured dividends are taxable. These represent payments to compensate buyers of securities for loss of dividend due, for instance, to late delivery of purchased shares.

Deep gain securities

Tax under Sch. D, Case III is payable on the discount obtained from deep gain securities when the amount payable on the redemption of a bond exceeds the issue price by more then ½% per annum or 15% in total and when the timing and amount of the redemption is uncertain. The income tax payable reduces the capital gains tax payable on the redemption of the securities. The rules do not apply where redemption can be enforced on the default (e.g. insolvency) of the issuer.

Capital gains

For treatment of capital gains and the inheritance tax in respect of investment see Chapter 5 of this book.

3.2 PERSONAL EQUITY PLANS (PEPs)

With effect from 6 April 1999 the PEP scheme was discontinued. After 6 April 1999 an existing PEP investment can continue to be held with the same tax advantages as an ISA, but no new contributions can be made to it. Also, contrary to the initial announcement following the 1998 budget, you *can* change your PEP provider after this date.

After 6 April 1999, prior PEP investments can be transferred into the Individual Savings Account (ISA), without affecting the normal ISA investment limits – see **3.4** below.

For the five-year period 6 April 1999–5 April 2004 the tax credit on dividends from PEP shares is reduced to 10% (the same credit rate as applicable to dividends from ISA investments).

3.3 INTEREST RECEIVABLE

General

Interest receivable forms part of the total income of all taxpayers, including individuals, companies and other bodies liable to tax. In most cases income tax at 20% is deducted, or assumed to be deducted, by the payer, and this system applies with some exceptions to government securities, debentures, other quoted stock and loans generally. If the recipient of the interest is not liable to pay tax the amount deducted can be reclaimed from the Inland Revenue. From 6 April 1999, if the top band is 10%, the difference can be reclaimed. Claims for repayment of tax at £50 or over can be made before the end of the year.

Interest gross of tax

In the following cases the interest is receivable without deduction of tax:

- On National Savings accounts – see below.
- From the Post Office.
- On off-shore accounts, e.g. those in the Isle of Man and the Channel Islands, and when received by persons not ordinarily resident in the UK.
- When application is made (on form R85) by a non-taxpayer for bank and building society interest to be paid gross. Severe penalties apply to false declarations.

Basis of assessment

Tax is now based on the amount of interest received in the tax year.

Payment of tax on interest

In most cases the taxpayer's liability for lower and basic rate tax on interest received will be satisfied by deduction of tax from the payment, the payer having to account to the Inland Revenue for the tax so deducted. Where interest is paid gross the taxpayer is liable to pay tax on the interest on 31 January in the year of assessment. However, for employees and pensioners the tax liability is usually met by the appropriate deduction from the allowances given in the coding. This adjustment to the coding is normally estimated so that a further coding adjustment may be necessary when the actual interest is known, or a refund of tax may be due.

For the purpose of calculating the taxpayer's liability to higher rate tax interest paid net of tax will be grossed up, and the excess over the basic rate will be payable on 31 January following the end of the year of assessment.

National Savings

(a) Ordinary Account. Up to £70 of interest from ordinary Savings Bank accounts is exempt from all rates of income tax.

(b) Investment Account. A higher rate of interest is payable than on the ordinary account but the interest is taxable, although tax is not deducted at source. Attractive to charities and individuals not liable to tax (who can apply for interest to be paid gross). One month's notice is required for withdrawal.

(c) National Savings Certificates and National Savings Bonds. A variety of issues have been made with tax-free interest.

(d) Save as You Earn. This is a system by which the saver contracts to make regular monthly contributions from £5 up to £150 a month to the National Savings Bank, the Trustee Savings Bank, other banks or certain building societies. A bonus, payable after certain stated periods, is tax free. At the end of three years savers have the option of taking the amount accrued in cash or buying shares in their company at a price set three years earlier, and this price can be discounted by up to 20%.

In 1995/96 ordinary save-as-you-earn contracts were abolished but tax relief continues for those linked to share options.

(e) Premium Savings Bonds. The maximum holding is £20 000 and prize money is tax-free.

(f) Government Stock on the National Savings Stock Register. The interest is paid without deduction of tax but is taxable in the recipient's hands.

(g) National Savings Pensioners Guaranteed Income Bond. The second issue of this bond is available to people aged 60 and over from 29 November 1995 and will pay monthly interest at fixed rates guaranteed for five years. Maximum holding is £50 000.

Tax-Exempt Special Savings Accounts (TESSA)

As with PEPs the TESSA scheme was discontinued with effect 6 April 1999. No new TESSA accounts will be opened after this date. However, normal subscriptions can continue over the five-year life of any TESSA opened prior to this date. In addition, any sum invested will be transferable into the new Individual Savings Accounts (ISA) – see **3.4** below.

TESSA accounts pay tax-free interest provided the capital is not withdrawn for five years, but the interest can be paid to the saver. The account must not be a joint account nor held on behalf of another person. The maximum investment is £3 000 in the first year, £1 800 a year for three years thereafter and £600 in the fifth year, giving a maximum investment of £9 000. Only one such account may be opened by an individual, who must not be under 18 years of age, but the balance may be transferred from one institution to another. After five years the continuing interest will be taxable but no liability to tax arises when an account is withdrawn on the death of the depositor.

The first TESSAs matured on 1 January 1996, being 5 years after 1 January 1991. The 1994 Budget provided that the capital of maturing TESSAs, up to a maximum of £9 000, but excluding accumulated interest, may be reinvested in a second account of which the interest will be tax-free for a further 5 years. The second account must be opened within 6 months of the maturity of the first account. The limits for a first deposit in a TESSA remains at £3 000 plus annual increases of £1 800. The bodies able to offer TESSAs are extended to authorised European authority institutions.

Savings with friendly societies

The 1994 Budget raised the maximum annual premium from £200 to £270 payable to friendly societies under tax-exempt life assurance policies. The tax-exempt surrender value is payable out of a tax-exempt fund after 10 years (or 7½ years for certain shorter-term policies) and need not be limited to a return of the premiums. These policies can represent tax-efficient forms of saving, especially for children under the age of 18.

3.4 INDIVIDUAL SAVINGS ACCOUNTS (ISAs)

This is a savings vehicle designed to make more people save. Its stated aim is to help the poor save. From 6 April 1999, it replaced new PEPs and TESSAs.

The main details are as follows:

- The tax benefits are guaranteed to last for at least 10 years.
- The returns are free from tax.
- There is no statutory minimum holding period or minimum subscription level.
- Qualifying investments are in 3 groups:
  - bank and building society accounts, and National Savings products
  - stocks and shares
  - life assurance.
- Normal annual subscription limit of £5 000 in total (£7 000 in 1999/00 and 2000/01), subject to:
  - maximum £1 000 in cash (£3 000 in 1999/00 and 2000/01)

  - maximum £1 000 invested in life assurance
  - balance in stocks and shares, to maximum of £5 000 (£7 000 in 1999/00 and 2000/01)
- The existence of a PEP investment made prior to 6 April does not affect the ISA limits.
- Continuing subscription over the five-year life of a TESSA account opened prior to 6th April 1999 (see **3.2** above) will not affect the annual subscription limit to an ISA.
- Capital from a maturing TESSA can be invested in an ISA without affecting the annual subscription limit.
- For the five-year period 6 April 1999–5 April 2004, a 10% tax credit will be paid on dividends from UK companies in respect of shares held in either an ISA or a PEP.

Other facts:

- One company can run all aspects of the ISA (maxi) for an individual, or alternatively different companies (mini) can run the respective cash, stocks and life assurance elements separately.
- Cash can be withdrawn any time without penalty but cannot be replaced if the cash limit was already reached previously.
- No lifetime limit applies.
- Shares from de-mutualised companies cannot be bought into an ISA.
- There will not be a prize draw as suggested when the scheme was first launched.

3.5 PROFIT SHARING

General

Companies operate various schemes allowing their employees, including directors, to obtain shares and share in profits in those companies on favourable terms. The employees may be offered options to acquire shares at below market prices; they may obtain the shares through Save As You Earn contracts; they may obtain interests in shares through trusts set up for the purpose; or they may be allotted shares individually. In addition profit-related pay schemes initiated in 1987 will be phased out by the year 2000. Many conditions apply to all these schemes for tax purposes but the general effect of the legislation is outlined as follows.

Share incentive schemes

These are schemes under which employees and directors are given the right to acquire shares in their employing company or another company (not in connection with a public issue) at a price below the market value. The director or employee is liable to tax under Schedule E on the excess of the market value at the earliest of the following dates over the market value at the date of acquiring the shares. The relevant dates are:

- Seven years after acquiring the shares;
- When the shares are sold;
- When the employment ceases, whether by death of the employee or director or otherwise;
- When the shares cease to be subject to restrictions.

The increase in value is taxable when it is due to:

- Improvements in the rights attaching to the shares or a restriction in the rights of other shares;
- Special benefits received by the employee or director, such as bonus issues, rights issues, vouchers or tokens exchangeable for goods or services, provided these benefits are not received by all the holders of the shares.

These increases in value do not apply for employee-controlled companies, nor to subsidiaries (but not dependent subsidiaries, i.e. whose business is mainly carried on with group members).

In the case of employees earning over £8 500 a year and directors the excess of the market value over the cost at the time of acquisition is treated as an interest-free loan, and tax is payable on interest at a commercial rate until the shares are sold or the taxpayer dies.

When the shares are sold capital gains tax will be payable on the increase in value which has not been charged on the employee for income tax.

Share options

Where an option is granted to a director or employee by reason of an office or employment there will generally be a charge to tax not when the option is granted, but when it is exercised. The charge will then be on the difference between the amount received and the amount paid (both for the shares and for the option itself). A charge to tax may, however, arise on the grant of the option where the employee is not within Case I of Schedule E, or where the option can be exercised more than 7 years after it was granted.

Liability to tax on the option can be avoided if the option is granted under one of the two Inland Revenue Approved Share Option Schemes.

SAYE share option scheme

This scheme gives employees the right to buy shares at a fixed price, using the proceeds of SAYE (Save As You Earn) savings contracts. The savings contract is made with a building society or bank, extended by the 1994 Finance Act to European authorised credit institutions. Tax relief is available only where new contracts are linked to share options. The price of the shares will be fixed at the time the option is granted, and the price must not be less than 80% of the market value of the shares at that time.

Employees do not have to use their options – this will depend on whether the shares increase in value over the period of the savings contract. If they do not use their options they will still receive the proceeds of their SAYE contract (tax free) when the contract matures.

Under the SAYE contract the employee saves a regular amount between £5 and £150 per month for 3, 5 or 7 years. The savings will stop after the contract period, but the contract may provide for the savings, plus bonus, to be paid. For the 'F Series' available from April 1993 the bonus after 5 years represents 9 times the monthly payments or 5.53% (previously 12.5 times or 7.5%), and after 7 years, 18 times the monthly payments or 5.87% (previously 25 times the monthly payments or 7.83%).

A scheme will only be approved by the Revenue if the shares used satisfy certain conditions to ensure that they are ordinary shares, and if the scheme is made available to all employees under similar terms.

If the scheme is approved the employee will not pay any income tax on:

- the benefit of being given an option to buy shares at a favourable price;
- any increase in the value of the shares between the date the option was given and the date on which it is used.

When the shares are sold any profit may still be charged to capital gains tax.

The maximum grant of new options is limited to £20 000.

Executive share option scheme

This scheme provides similar tax reliefs to the SAYE Share Option Scheme. However, it is not linked to a savings contract, and does not have to be operated for all employees on similar terms.

To qualify for tax reliefs the option must be held for at least 3 and no more than 10 years, and only one option exercise can qualify for relief in any 3-year period. The scheme must also be approved by the Inland Revenue before any options are granted under it.

Only full-time directors and employees working at least 20 hours per week can participate, and there are limits on the size of options which can be granted. Following perceived abuse, new rules apply to options granted on or after 17 July 1995 limiting new options to £20 000 per employee.

Profit sharing through shares

There is a further scheme which can be approved by the Inland Revenue, which offers special tax reliefs when shares are acquired by employees. This scheme requires the company concerned to set up a trust fund. The company then makes cash payments to the trustees to buy shares in the company. The trustees then set aside some of these shares for each employee who takes part in the scheme.

Qualifying corporate bonds, issued to trustees on a reconstruction or take-over of a company can, after the Finance Act 1993, be retained by the trustees and in due course be passed tax free to participants in the scheme.

The scheme must be available to all qualifying employees on similar terms. The shares cannot generally be taken out of the trust for two years, and if the acquisition of the shares is to be completely free of tax the shares should not be taken out until after five years.

There are complex rules on the operation of the scheme, on the types of shares which can be used, and on the maximum amount which can be allocated to each employee.

Employee share ownership plans (ESOPs)

The ESOP scheme is distinct from the above schemes. It is operated by an all-employee trust which receives payments from a company for the purpose of buying that company's shares on behalf of employees. These payments are tax deductible by the company if made within nine months (subject to extension) and claimed within two years from the end of the accounting period concerned. The trust can also borrow money for the purpose of buying the shares. Within seven years of acquiring the shares the trust must distribute them to employees on equal terms. There is no limit to the number of shares which the trust can acquire out of its funds.

These plans could be attractive to a company which wishes to encourage employee ownership of its shares, and the donations which the company makes to the trust would give relief from corporation tax. Setting-up costs are allowable from 1 April 1991. The employees would eventually receive their equal allocation of the shares without payment, but would then be liable to income tax on the value so received. The trust would be liable to income tax and capital gains tax on its income, but tax benefits might be gained if the ESOP trust transferred the shares to a profit-sharing scheme.

From 20 March 1990 capital gains made on the transfer of shares to the trust can be rolled over, i.e. set off against replacement assets, where the trust has a 10% interest in the company within 12 months of the sale of the shares and replacement assets are acquired within six months.

In addition to the above schemes, two further schemes were announced in the March 2000 Budget.

Profit-related pay (PRP) was abolished from 1 January 2000

All employee share plan

- Employers can give employees up to £3 000 of shares each year free of tax and National Insurance.
- Some or all of these shares can be awarded to employees for reaching performance targets.
- Employees will be able to buy partnership shares out of their pre-tax salary up to a maximum of £1 500 a year, free of tax and National Insurance. Employees who keep their shares in the plan for 5 years will pay no income tax or National Insurance in respect of these shares.
- If the shares are only kept in the plan for 3 years, tax and National Insurance is paid on the initial value - any increase being tax free.
- If the employees retain the shares in the plan until disposal, they will not be liable to Capital Gains Tax.
- Companies will get corporation tax relief on costs they incur in providing shares for employees to buy, to the extent that such costs exceed the employee's contributions.
- Shares held in qualifying employee share ownership trusts on Budget Day can be transferred into a new plan trust without losing the corporation tax already given.
- Companies can award free shares in respect of performance periods that begin before the Finance Bill 2000 becomes law.
- As a transitional measure, companies can run an approved profit sharing scheme alongside a new plan that provides partnership shares, although no further tax free awards will be able to be made after April 2002.
- Up to £1 500 of dividends may be reinvested in shares tax free each year within the trust.
- Employees and trustees will have freedom to make their own arrangements about transferring shares when an employee leaves.
- There is a new capital gains tax rollover relief to existing shareholders who want to sell their shares to a new plan trust to be used for the benefit of employees.
- The existence of arrangements to enable employees to sell shares in a new plan trust will not of itself make those shares readily convertible into cash, requiring the employers to operate PAYE and account for National Insurance.

Companies will be able to send in draft plans for approval under a fast-track approvals system.

Enterprise Management Incentive Scheme

- Independent trading companies with gross assets not exceeding £15 million will be able to award up to 15 key employees (previously announced as 10) with tax advantaged share options, each receiving options worth up to £100 000 at the time of grant.
- There is no tax charge on the grant of the option and there will be normally no tax or National Insurance for the employee to pay when the options are exercised; nor will there normally be any National Insurance charge for the employer.

When shares are sold, CGT taper relief will normally start from the date the options are granted.

3.6 BUSINESS EXPANSION SCHEME

This scheme, which was terminated in December 1993, gave income tax relief from the cost of shares taken up in certain new companies carrying on new trades. It was replaced by the Enterprise Investment Scheme – see below.

3.7 ENTERPRISE INVESTMENT SCHEME (EIS)

This investment scheme replaced the Business Expansion Scheme on 1 January 1994 when the latter terminated in December 1993. The main factors of the scheme are as follows:

- Unquoted trading companies trading but not necessarily resident or incorporated in the UK can from 6 April 1998 raise unlimited capital by shares issued under the scheme (previously £1m per year) subject to gross assets being less than £10 million before the investment and £11 million after. The limit is £5m a year for shipping activities. Companies investing in private rented housing are not qualified for the scheme. Approved investment funds are covered.
- Investors can subscribe for EIS shares up to £150,000 from 6 April 1998 (previously £100,000).
- The investment in an EIS scheme gives tax relief at 20% and capital gains tax exemption on the first disposal of the shares. The shares must be held for five years. Half the investment made between 6 April and 5 October in any year, up to a maximum of £25 000 from 6 April 1998 (previously £15 000), can be carried back to the previous tax year.
- Qualifying investors must not be employees or shareholders of the company owning more than 30% of the shares, but subsequent to the issue of the shares an investor can become a paid director, retaining the right to the tax relief.

A further increase to assist small businesses are Venture Capital Trusts, investors in unquoted trading companies, giving tax-free dividends and capital gains. Various conditions apply to these trusts.

The following improvements to the scheme were announced in the 1998 Budget:

- Guaranteed loans will no longer form part of the fixed proportion of qualifying investments which a VCT must hold if individual investors are to benefit from the tax reliefs.
- VCTs will be required to ensure that at least 10% of their total investment in any company is held in ordinary non-preferential shares.

These changes apply to VCTs for accounting periods ending on or after 2 July 1997 but not in respect of funds raised by the issue of shares before 2 July 1997.

This is in addition to the existing rules which are as follows:

- Tax relief will be available when a chargeable gain after is reinvested in an EIS. The tax relief will be at 20% on the investment as well as capital gains exemption. The relief is available when the investment in EIS shares is made one year before and up to three years after the capital gain is realised. The gain will be brought back into charge if the company ceases to be a qualifying company.
- Individuals who belong to groups of persons cannot obtain the relief for investment in companies which they control.
- Individuals may obtain the relief of tax when they invest in companies which subsequently make rights issues at discount.
- Capital gains exemption will be available when the company in which the investment is made after five years merges with another EIS or BES company.
- A loss on the disposal or shares is an allowable loss for capital gains tax.
- The capital gains tax relief is restricted to the extent that the investing shareholder receives value from the company.

3.8 SCRIP DIVIDENDS

Where a taxpayer opts to take a dividend in the form of shares or stock, instead of cash, the dividend will be grossed up at the lower rate of income tax. The gross amount will be chargeable to higher rates of income tax if applicable. The market value may apply if higher than the cash equivalent.

3.9 UNIT TRUSTS

Authorised unit trusts and investment trusts are exempt from capital gains tax after 31 January 1980. In the case of those trusts with specific instructions as to their operations, income from investment in gilt-edged stock is liable to basic rate income tax and not corporation tax. In both cases the holder will be liable to capital gains tax on the disposal of his or her holding, subject to normal exemptions. Regulations under the Charities Act 1992, effective on 1 January 1993, enable charitable unit trusts to transmit income to participating charities without deduction of tax.

When authorised under company law, open-ended investment companies (OEIC) will fall under the same provisions as apply to unit trusts. Open-ended investment companies are those where their shares are continuously created or redeemed.

3.10 Offshore Funds

The offshore funds legislation applies to a wide range of investment vehicles set up overseas, often in the form of open-ended investment companies or unit trusts. If a significant proportion of the income is distributed to investors, the capital gains on the disposal of the investment is liable to capital gains tax. Where capital gains are rolled up in the fund the investors are charged income tax on the disposal of their holdings.

CHAPTER 4

BUSINESS TAXATION

4.1 THE SYSTEM SUMMARISED

The assessment

The profits from trading and professional activities are assessed under Cases I and II of Schedule D and profits from other sources may be assessable under the other Schedules and Cases. This chapter is particularly concerned with assessments under Cases I and II of Schedule D.

In strictness, none of the personal reliefs and allowances reviewed in the previous chapters of this book is applicable to a business assessment as such. But where the business is unincorporated, i.e. owned by one person or a partnership, the reliefs and allowances applicable to the owners may be set off against their share of the business assessment. A limited company is, however, a 'legal person' and the tax assessment made on its own profits is not subject to the reliefs due to the owners, that is the shareholders, even if it is effectively owned by one person.

Unincorporated businesses

The profits of a business owned by one individual or a partnership are liable to income tax. The amount so payable may be reduced by the owners' reliefs and allowances. It may be, however, that all of an individual taxpayer's reliefs are set off against income other than the profits from his or her business, and this situation should normally occur where the taxpayer was in a salaried employment as well as running a business. In the case of a partnership a return of the partnership computation must be made on behalf of the firm and the individual partners must make returns of their own incomes, including that received from the partnership. The tax payable is due by the individual partners in the agreed profit-sharing ratios.

Incorporated businesses

So far as most limited companies and many other corporate bodies are concerned, their taxable profits are subject to corporation tax and not income tax.

From 6 April 1999, no ACT (Advance Corporation Tax) is deducted prior to the issue of a dividend. Funds must be kept available for the payment of the tax liability nine months after the company's year end.

The dividend in the hands of the shareholder comes with a non-refundable tax credit at 10%.

Whether the business is incorporated or not the profits which it shows in its accounts will almost always need adjustment for the purpose of arriving at the profit figure on which tax is payable. This aspect of the subject is considered in the next section.

4.2 ADJUSTING THE ACCOUNTS PROFIT

General – the basis of adjustment

The profit shown in the accounts of a business, whether it is incorporated or not, is adjusted for tax purposes (a) by adding back expenses disallowed, and (b) by deducting income which is not taxable. The resulting assessment may then be reduced by capital allowances, and loss relief. The question as to whether a particular item is allowable or not is sometimes difficult to determine, and is a frequent cause of appeal to the Commissioners and to the Courts. For profits arising from trading, which are assessed under Cases I and II of Schedule D, the over-riding rules are that expenditure must (a) be wholly and exclusively incurred for the purpose of the trade or profession, and (b) not be of a capital nature.

Expenses disallowed

The following expenses are not allowed in the tax computation – that is, they must be added back to the accounts profits or deducted from an accounts loss:

- Expenses not arising out of the trade or profession, e.g. medical fees.
- Withdrawals of capital and profits, e.g. by dividends, proprietors' or partners' shares of profit or salaries (but salaries payable to directors of limited companies are normally allowable).
- Capital expenditure, such as extensions or improvements to premises, legal expenses connected with capital expenditure, company formation expenses, and capital losses (but see also under Capital Gains).
- Depreciation. Capital allowances (see below) may be available in place of depreciation.
- Personal expenditure of proprietors such as personal life insurance premiums and private usage of business cars.
- Annual payments from which tax has been deducted, where the business is unincorporated and pays income tax.
- Appropriations of profit such as dividends, reserves and taxation.
- General provisions for bad debts, e.g. by applying a percentage, but reasonable provisions against specific debtors and actual bad debts are allowed.

- Entertainment expenses and gifts. Relief for entertainment of foreign customers was abolished in 1988/89. However, the general rule is relaxed for gifts to employees and gifts to any one person in a year costing no more than £10 from 5 April 1985 (previously £2) and incorporating advertising matter.
- Cost of appealing against income tax assessments; and accountants' fees in connection with an Inland Revenue investigation.
- Penalties for breaches of the law.
- Deductions for self-cancelling annuities representing tax avoidance schemes were not allowable (Moodie v IRC 1993 HL following W. T. Ramsey v CIR 1982, AC).

Allowable expenses

In general, business expenses which do not fall under the foregoing prohibitions are allowable for tax purposes but the following allowable expenses are worthy of special mention:

- Repairs and maintenance of trade premises, plant, fittings, vehicles, etc., not being of the nature of additions or improvements. Renewals are not allowed if capital allowances are claimed.
- Rent and rates of trade or professional premises. Where part of a private residence is exclusively used for the business a proportion of the rent and a proportion of any premium may be claimed. This proportion may be based on floor area.
- Employees' remuneration, directors' fees, employer's National Insurance contributions and contributions to approved superannuation funds payable by the business. The self-employed cannot charge their own National Insurance contributions against their profits.
- Business insurance premiums, but sums received under claims must be brought into account as well as the expense.
- Travelling expenses wholly and exclusively incurred for the purpose of the business, but note that employees earning £8 500 and directors may have to justify reimbursed expenses and expense allowances. Travelling expenses include reasonable hotel expenses necessarily incurred.
- Losses from theft, but see under insurance above.
- Advertising, if not of a capital nature.
- Dilapidations payable on terminations of leases to the extent that the payment represents deferred repairs.
- Losses;on exchange as they accrue if clearly a risk of the trade. Consideration will be given to allowing, or treating as income, exchange differences on monetary assets and, from 6 April 1993, these differences are not subject to capital gains tax.
- Compensation to employees arising out of their terms of service; also voluntary pensions and gratuities on retirement. Redundancy

payments and additions thereto up to three times the amount of the redundancy payment.

- Bank interest payable by limited companies, provided it is a proper business expense. Interest paid by the self-employed may have to be apportioned between business and private use.
- On and after 1 April 1980, the incidental costs of obtaining loans or issuing loan stock.
- Pre-trading expenditure for trades, professions, etc. Businesses beginning trading on and after 1 April 1993 may claim relief for expenditure incurred up to the previous seven years. The relief extends to certain interest and the preparation of sites for waste disposal, but note that a 'Land fill' tax was proposed in the November 1994 Budget.
- Contributions to certain 'enterprise agencies' for 10 years from 31 March 1982. The agencies include LEA's, TEC's, LEC's and from 30 November 1993 Business Links.
- Salaries of staff lent to charities and approved educational establishments.
- Discount and incidental costs of issuing bills of exchange accepted by banks.
- Employees' expenses on approved retraining courses, including sandwich courses, within the UK and for up to a year. The expenses include lodging, subsistence, books and travelling. The employee must have two years' service with the employer; the facility must be available to all employees of a similar class; and the course must start during employment or two years thereafter. The limit was raised to £7 000 a year from 6 April 1992
- Gifts of equipment to schools and other educational establishments (1991/92), and other charitable gifts.
- The cost of setting up employee share schemes and ESOPs (1991/92).
- Accountancy expenses in preparing accounts and negotiating routine tax liabilities, but not those for Inland Revenue investigations which reveal that profits have not been fully declared.
- Cost of food and a proportion of business accommodation when working away from home (Prior v Saunders 1993).

Assessable income

Fewer problems arise with regard to the income or credit side of the profit and loss account of a business. The major part of business income in the form of sales to customers or fees charged to clients needs no adjustment for tax purposes. The following, however, merit particular mention:

- Capital profits on the sale of fixed assets will affect capital allowances and may be subject to the capital gains tax provisions, but are not otherwise taxable.

- Casual profits are normally assessable either under Cases I or II or under Case VI of Schedule D.
- Betting profits are not normally assessable unless made by a bookmaker but the mere fact that a transaction is of the nature of a speculation does not automatically make it exempt from tax.
- Exchange profits will be assessable if arising out of the trade carried on.
- Profits from illegal trading are assessable.
- Rent receivable from unfurnished letting is normally assessable as it accrues from 10 March 1992.
- Grants under the Industry Act 1972, except where the grant is for capital expenditure or compensation for loss of capital assets – after 26 March 1980.

Income not assessable

Some part of the income shown in the accounts of businesses may not be assessable for income tax or corporation tax. This will usually be the case where the income is not derived from the trade carried on or where it is of a capital nature. In the case of income not derived from the trade under assessment it is, however, possible that the Inspector of Taxes may take the view that a new trade has been established and make an assessment on those grounds. Where income is of a capital nature – for example, a profit on the sale of plant – that profit may be subject to the capital gains provisions. Other examples of non-assessable income are as follows:

- Gifts received are not normally assessable, unless they consist of benefits to directors and higher-paid employees, and exceed £100 in a year.
- Damages receivable in a legal action are of a capital nature, and so is compensation, e.g. on cancellation of an agreement.
- Regional development grants.

PAYE and National Savings contributions

The amounts deducted from the remuneration of employees, including national insurance, are normally refunded to the Inland Revenue monthly. The payments, including National Insurance, can be made quarterly if they average less than £1 500 per month from 5 April 2000 (£1 000 per month previously).

4.3 A SPECIMEN COMPUTATION

The following specimen computation of a fictitious business is intended to illustrate a selection of the points mentioned above. For simplicity the accounts of a partnership business are used as certain special considerations which are dealt with later apply to limited companies.

Essentially, however, the method is the same whatever the form of the business concerned.

A and B in partnership
TRADING AND PROFIT AND LOSS ACCOUNT
for the year ended 31 December 1999

			£
Sales, less returns and VAT			200 000
Less: cost of goods sold			120 000
GROSS PROFIT			80 000
Less: operating expenses			
Salaries:	£	£	
Partners	20 000		
Staff	18 000		
Total salaries		38 000	
National Insurance:			
Partners	2 200		
Staff	1 800		
Total Nat. Insurance		4 000	
Rent and rates	2 000		
Maintenance and improvement of premises	1 000		
Total premises expense		3 000	
Insurance:			
General	700		
Partners' life insurance	300		
Total insurance		1 000	
Travelling:			
Fares	300		
Subsistence	200		
Car expenses, incl. petrol, oil, depreciation & repairs	2 500		
Total travelling		3 000	
Entertainment		200	
Stationery & postage		400	
Advertising		800	
Donations & subscriptions:			
Local hospital	50		
Golf club	150		

Total donations		200	
Bad debts written off		300	
Provision for doubtful debts at 5% of debtors		1 200	
Depreciation of equipment		1 900	
Total operating expenses			54 000
Operating profit			£26 000
Add: **Non-trading income:**			
Insurance commission	150		
Profit on sale of van	350		
Total non-trading income			500
			26 500
Less: **Non-trading expenses:**			
Interest on loan, gross	1 420		
Interest on partners' capital	580		
Total non-trading expenses			2 000
PRETAX PROFIT			24 500
Less: Income tax provision			6 500
NET PROFIT AFTER TAX			£18 000

TAX COMPUTATION BASED ON THE ABOVE ACCOUNTS

	£	£	*Comments*
Profits per accounts before tax		24 500	Income tax is an appropriation of profit
Add back charges disallowed:			
Partners' salaries	20 000		Regarded as appropriation of profit; directors' salaries would normally be allowed if the business was a limited company.
Partners' Nat. Insurance	2 200		
Improvements to premises	500		A capital expense
Car expenses	130		Disallowed for private use – see text for details of method.

Partners' life assurance	300		A personal expense
Entertainment	200		
Golf club sub	150		Probably not wholly and necessarily expended for business purposes; the amount for the local hospital may be allowed.
Provision for doubtful debts	1 200		Only the write-off against specific debts is allowable.
Depreciation	1 900		Capital allowances are available instead.
Interest on loan	1 420		Possibly subject to deduction of tax at source.
Interest on partners' capital	580		An appropriation of profit.
		28 580	
		53 080	
Deduct income not chargeable:			
Profit on sale of van		350	Capital – will affect capital allowances
Taxable profit		£52 730	

The taxable profit would be reduced by capital allowances and loss relief, and would be apportioned to the partners in their profit-sharing ratios. The amount so apportioned would then form part of each partner's personal computation.

Rounding of business computations

Subject to some qualifications the Inland Revenue are prepared to accept business computations of profits rounded to the nearest £1 000. This applies where such rounding is applied to the business accounts and turnover is not less than £5 million. In particular rounding does not apply to: chargeable gains (except for incidental costs of acquisition and disposal); tax credit relief for overseas companies; accrued income and most computations of capital allowances (PR 18 May 1993).

4.4 CAPITAL ALLOWANCES

Meaning and purpose of 'capital allowances'

The figure for the depreciation of fixed assets which is charged in the accounts of a business is not allowable for tax purposes. Instead of depreciation various 'capital allowances' may be deducted from the assessed profits. Many people are confused as to why depreciation is not allowed but capital allowances are. The depreciation figure in the accounts is an accounting adjustment calculated to progressively write off the assets over their useful lives (producing a "fair and reasonable" representation of the actual value of the Company's assets). Capital allowances represent the amount of write-off which is allowed *for tax purposes* – normally *greater* than the depreciation amount for the first few years, particularly in the first year. The (faster) rate at which an asset can be written down *for tax purposes* bears no relation to the actual value or life of the assets concerned; it is a governmental concession designed to stimulate capital investment by offering the carrot of higher tax relief in the year of purchase. In effect the tax reliefs are all skewed towards the front end of the asset life, so that instead of having an even progression of tax reliefs, they are mostly taken in the early years, resulting in lower tax in those earlier years and correspondingly higher tax in later years. For the purpose of the accounts, the assets are recorded at their fair value, not their artificially low "tax-written-down" value, and the amount of tax initially saved (or, in effect, deferred) as a result of the accelerated write-down is recorded in the accounts as "deferred tax".

Capital allowances apply to industrial buildings, ships, mines, oil wells, plant and machinery. The term 'plant and machinery' covers a wide field and includes vehicles, furniture, fixtures and fittings for business purposes.

Capital allowances are applicable only to plant and machinery belonging to the trader, but the payment of a deposit indicates ownership. If the expenditure becomes abortive, disposal value will apply.

There are essentially four groups of capital allowances: first-year allowances, initial allowances, writing-down allowances (formerly known as 'annual allowances' or 'wear and tear allowances') and balancing allowances or balancing charges.

First-year allowances

These allowances apply to plant and machinery (defined widely) and represent a percentage of the cost when the expenditure was incurred and the asset acquired. Having been abolished in 1986, they were reintroduced at a rate of 50% and for the year 2 July 1998–1 July 2000 at a rate of 40%. The March 2000 budget made this first year allowance of 40% permanent. It is available to businesses defined as small and medium (See below.) Except for capital expenditure on research and development (not including buildings) where the allowance is 100% of cost. For Northern Ireland only, a first-year allowance of 100% is allowed on assets bought by small and medium-sized businesses (as defined below). This runs from 12 May 1998 to 11 May 2002.

Small businesses that invest in Information and Communications Technology equipment (computers, software and Internet-enabled mobile phones) over 3 years from 1 April 2000, will be able to claim 100% first year allowances.

The first-year allowances are only available to small and/or medium-sized businesses as defined as satisfying 2 of the 3 following conditions for the current or previous year (current year only in the case of companies):

Small	Medium
• turnover less than £2.8 million	• turnover less than £11.2 million
• assets less than £1.4 million	• assets less than £5.6 million
• not more than 50 employees	• not more than 250 employees

They do not apply to expenditure on machinery and plant for leasing or letting on hire, cars, long-life assets, sea-going ships and railway assets. These must rely on the standard "writing-down allowances" referred to below.

After the first-year allowance has been taken, where applicable, subsequent write-down allowances are provided by "writing-down allowances" for the following years (see below).

Initial allowances

Initial allowances were calculated on cost and were additional to writing-down allowances (see below) also calculated on cost in the first year. They applied generally to expenditure on industrial and commercial buildings but, subject to the exceptions indicated below, were abolished for expenditure after 31 March 1986. The cases where the allowances continue to apply include expenditure on industrial and commercial buildings, including shops and offices, in Enterprise Zones. The allowance is 100% of cost including VAT unless a writing-down allowance of 25% on cost is claimed instead.

Writing-down allowances

(a) Plant and machinery. The standard writing down-allowance on plant and machinery ("long life assets") is 25% for annual expenditure not exceeding £100,000, reduced to 6%, from 26 November 1996, if annual expenditure exceeds £100,000.

The writing-down allowance is an annual allowance calculated on the balance of a "pool" of the cost or written-down values of all applicable assets. There is a pool for plant and machinery generally and a separate pool for business cars (used for business only). This requirement for a separate pool for cars costing less than £12,000 will be abolished from the present chargeable period. That is the chargeable period that includes 1 April 2000 for corporation tax and 6 April 2000 for income tax. A balance brought forward on the existing pool will be added to the main pool. Cars with any element of private use have to be treated separately as referred to below. The maximum writing-down allowance on individual cars costing over £12 000 is £3 000 p.a. The pooling system began on 5 April 1976 when the written-down balances of the then existing assets of a business were aggregated. The balance in the pool is increased by the cost of assets purchased and decreased by the proceeds from any assets sold as well as by the writing-down allowance for each year. The 1986 Finance Act included provisions for depooling of shorter-life assets, other than cars or ships, with lives of up to four years and acquired on or after 1 April 1986.

Example

	£
Written-down balance in pool at beginning of year	10 000
Add: purchases of assets in year (Oct 1999)	4 000
	14 000
Less: sale proceeds of assets in year	2 000
	12 000
First-year allowance – £4 000 x 40%	1 600
Writing-down allowance for the year – £8 000 x 25%	2 000
Written-down balance at end of year	8 400

Where assets are fully written off by the 100% first-year allowance they are obviously not eligible for any writing-down allowance in addition. For assets not subject to the first-year allowance the writing-down allowance can be claimed in the year of purchase.

(b) Industrial buildings, agricultural buildings and hotels. The writing-down allowance is 4% applied each year to the cost, including the first year, and is deducted from the written-down balance as well as the first-year allowance, where applicable. To qualify for the allowance a hotel must have at least 10 bedrooms, be open to the public for at least four months in a year and provide breakfast and an evening meal as part of the normal service. Where industrial buildings are leased for over 50 years the lessee can claim the allowance provided there is a joint election by both lessor and lessee.

The rate of writing-down allowance for agricultural buildings is also 4% from 1 April 1986 (previously 10%). From 1 April 1986, a system of balancing adjustments operates at the taxpayer's option when a building is demolished or sold. In 1982/83 the allowance was extended to include buildings used for certain repairing and servicing activities. For expenditure after 19 June 1989 the agricultural buildings allowance no longer applies to forestry land.

From 6 April 1995 capital allowances could be claimed for private investment in public roads, including toll roads.

(c) Private cars used for business. These have to be accounted for individually (not in a pool), and a writing-down allowance of 25% is allowable on each vehicle, each year. The amount of the allowance which is set off against tax will depend on the proportion of business/private use. The maximum claimable per car per annum before splitting between private and business is £3 000.

(d) Miscellaneous. For expenditure on patents or 'know-how' allowances are provided from 31 March 1986 at 25% on the reducing balance. Special provisions apply to ships, mines and oil wells. The 1992 Finance Act (2) extended capital allowances to capital expenditure on computer software licences and software distributed by electronic means. Capital allowances already apply to purchases of these assets.

Balancing allowances and balancing charges

These allowances or charges apply in the year when the asset is sold or scrapped and their purpose is to ensure that no more nor less than the net cost of an asset, after deducting receipts from the eventual sale, is allowable as a charge against taxable profits. Where the pool system is in use the sale proceeds are deducted from the balance in the pool. If the sale proceeds are greater than the pool balance, the difference is a balancing charge, i.e. added to profit. If the sale proceeds exceed the cost, then a capital gain may arise on that excess. With the pool system balancing allowances normally arise only on cessation of a business but they may arise for 'depooled' short life assets. In addition items which have their own pool such as cars (greater than £12 000 cost) and assets with a proportion of private use will certainly lead to a balancing adjustment, unless disposed at written-down value.

Basis period

Capital allowances refer to the accounting year on which the assessment is based. The profits of a business in single ownership or a partnership would, for the accounts year to, say, 31 December 1999, normally be assessed for the tax year 1999/00. Capital allowances to be deducted from the assessment would refer to assets acquired in the year to 31 December 1999. But see also under section 4.6 below.

Replaced plant

Where a balancing charge arises on the disposal of an asset which is to be replaced, the taxpayer can elect to deduct the balancing charge from the cost of the new asset, but this would reduce allowances on the latter.

Leased plant

A writing down allowance of 25% can be claimed by trading lessors on plant obtained for leasing.

Income tax losses due to capital allowances and arising from leasing are not available for set-off against non-leasing income by individuals or partnerships, except a full-time leasing business carried on for at least six months.

The budget in March 2000 introduced a new rule which will enable allowances to be claimed by the lessor on the lower of cost to and sale by the lessee, provided certain conditions are met:

a) the equipment is new when acquired by the lessee
b) the acquision is not from a connected person, a sale and lease back or a 'main benefit' sale
c) the equipment is sold to the lessor not more tyan 4 months after it is firstbrought into usse and the lessee does not claim capital allowance.

Leased cars

Taxis, private hire cars and those hired out for short terms, or to disabled persons, qualify for writing-down allowances of 25% in the year of acquisition, with a limit to the cost of £12 000. Short term means hiring for no more than 30 days to a particular person, and for less than 90 days in 12 months.

The lessee can charge the whole cost of the rental for the car (assuming it is used for business purposes) provided the retail price was no more that £12 000. Where the retail price exceeds £12 000 the allowable charge in the lessee's computation is that proportion of the rental which is represented by the following fraction: £12 000 plus half the excess price over £12 000 divided by the price.

Hire purchase

The business which obtains plant by means of hire purchase may claim capital allowances on all capital expenditure (excluding the interest charge) incurred under the contract as though it had been incurred when the contract began.

Security assets

From 5 April 1989 expenditure by individuals or partnerships on business are eligible for capital allowances. These are assets provided to meet a special threat to an individual's security, but exclude cars, ships, aircraft and living accommodation.

Enterprise Zones

The Enterprise Zones scheme began in 1980 to encourage business in certain areas but further expansion of the scheme ceased in 1987. The scheme provides an initial allowance of 100% of expenditure on the construction, improvement or extension of industrial and commercial buildings in the zone. Alternatively a 25% straight-line annual writing-down allowance can be claimed. The construction must be incurred within ten years of the designation of an area as an Enterprise Zone, and also applies to expenditure incurred within ten years thereafter under a contract made within the original ten-year period. If the building was sold before being put into use the purchaser would receive the allowance, and would do so if the building was acquired within two years of being brought into use.

Films, discs and tapes

Expenditure on the production or acquisition of the original master version of a film, disc or tape (not reproductions) is regarded as revenue expenditure for tax purposes. Income from the exploitation of the film or master negatives is likewise regarded as of a revenue, not capital nature. The amount of the expenditure which can be written off in a period of account is divided either by the 'income matching method' or the 'cost recovery method'. By the first method the expenditure to be written off in a period of account is related to the proportion of the total estimated income received in that period, subsequent adjustments becoming necessary when total income is revised. The cost recovery method provides that, by a claim within two years of the end of a period of account, total expenditure in a period exactly equals the value realised.

4.5 TURNOVER UNDER £15 000

The Inland Revenue accepts simplified (3-line) accounts where the turnover is less than £15 000. This information is entered on the Self-Assessment tax return. The Accounts themselves need not be submitted as well.

The arrangement applies to individuals and partnerships, including those receiving rental income below the limit. These simplified accounts are limited to a statement of turnover less the total of the business expenses arrived at in accordance with the tax rules indicated above. Details of capital allowances claimed must also be stated on the return., and included in the expenses figure. The Tax Inspector may, however, call for further information, possibly full accounts, especially if a loss is shown or the business is subdivided so that each unit falls below the turnover limit. For these reasons, as well as for internal management purposes, it is always desirable for a small venture to have full accounts prepared and available.

4.6 UNINCORPORATED BUSINESSES/PARTNERSHIPS

Basis of assessment

From 1996/97, and retrospectively for businesses started after 5 April 1994, assessment is made on a 'current year basis', based on profits in the accounting year ending in the tax year of assessment.

Prior to 1996/97, for a business in sole ownership or partnership the assessment for income tax under Cases I and II of Schedule D was normally based on the adjusted profits made in the accounts year ending immediately before the tax year of assessment, known as 'the preceding year basis'. For pre 5 April 1994 businesses the accounts for the years ended in 1995/96 and 1996/97 were averaged in order to bring the business into the current year basis. This means that only half of the income were taxed, and only half of expenses were given tax relief.

In 1996/97 and onwards returns of partnership income are made by a 'representative partner' and assessed on the partnership. Individual partners are required to self-assess their total income, including that from the partnership.

Cessation

From 29 November 1994 certain trading expenses are eligible for tax relief after a business ceases and can be set off against the income and/or capital gains of the individual who pays such expenses. The expenditure concerned could include that which was closely related to the former business or professional activities such as: the cost of remedying defective work, insurance premiums and legal costs in connection with defective work, debts which have become bad debts after the cessation of the business and the costs of debt collection. No relief will be given where these expenses have been charged (e.g. by way of provisions) on the business accounts. The expenditure must be incurred within 7 years after the trade ceases and claims must be made within 2 years after the year of assessment in which the expense is paid.

Change of Partners

Where one or more members of a partnership leave the firm, and where new partners are introduced, the old partnership is theoretically discontinued and a new partnership is assumed to be set up. If at least one of the old partners remains, an election can be made for tax purposes within two years of the change to treat the firm as a continuing business.

Stock valuation on cessation

The valuation of stock when a business is sold or discontinued and transferred to a connected person must be as for an arm's-length transaction.

4.7 RELIEF FOR LOSSES

Basically, there are three ways of dealing with a business loss (which means a taxable loss after adjusting the accounts in the manner set out above).

Carry forward

The first, and perhaps the most usual, method, which applies to both unincorporated businesses and to limited companies, is to carry forward the loss and set it off against the next assessment. If the next assessment is insufficient to absorb the whole of the loss then the balance is carried forward to be set off against the following assessment and so on. There is no time limit except for 'hobby farmers', where the limit is six years. Capital allowances which cannot be deducted from an assessment because a loss has been incurred may also be carried forward indefinitely until they can be set off against profits.

In effect, therefore, capital allowances increase the loss. An individual starting in business is able to set a trading loss against profits or income of the three previous years. General income could include earnings from employment.

Carry back

The second method is to 'carry back' the losses. For an unincorporated business or partnership, where a loss occurred in any of the first three years of trading, that loss can be set off against profits or an individual's general income of the preceding three years, absorbing income of the earliest year first. For an incorporated business (i.e. a limited company) business losses can be carried back for one year and set off against the company's earlier profits.

Set-off

The third method of dealing with a business loss, which applies only to individuals and unincorporated businesses or partnerships, is to offset the loss incurred by an individual in business against the total statutory income for the year. If the total statutory income of a taxpayer for 1999/00 was £10 000 and he or she sustained a loss in his business of £1 700 for the financial year to 31 March 2000, the taxpayer could claim to have the £1 700 set off against the £10 000 and thus reduce the 1999/00 assessment to £8 300. A claim will be admitted only where the business which sustains the loss is carried on with a reasonable expectation of profit.

Capital gains

As regards an individual's loss in business, the 1991 Finance Act provided that so much of a loss as could not be recouped in the manner referred to above shall be treated as an allowable loss for capital gains tax, subject to official 'determination' of the amount, and to the business continuing.

4.8 COMPANIES AND CORPORATION TAX

Limited company

Limited companies and other corporate bodies are assessed for corporation tax on the profits, adjusted for tax purposes, made in the company's accounting year.

Scope and nature of the tax

Limited companies as well as most other corporate bodies and some trading clubs and unincorporated associations are liable to pay corporation tax, but not income tax, on their profits as adjusted for tax purposes. Unincorporated businesses, owned by individuals or partnerships, are assessed for income tax. Dividends paid by companies do not reduce the profit assessable to corporation tax, but up to 5 April 1999 the income tax 'imputed' to the dividend was charged to the Company by way of Advance Corporation Tax (ACT). This ACT could then be offset by reducing the corporation tax charged on the Company's profits, or carried back if the ACT was greater than the corporation tax chargeable. See **Advance Corporation Tax** below.

Advance Corporation Tax (ACT) – Ceased 6 April 1999

As referred to above, up to 5 April 1999 income tax on a Company's dividends was 'imputed' and charged to the Company by way of 'Advance Corporation Tax' (ACT). The income tax was imputed at a rate of 20% on the implied gross dividend – i.e. 25% of the net amount paid (20/80) – and the company accounted to the Inland Revenue for this tax on a quarterly basis. (For details of the income tax treatment of the dividends received by shareholders see section 3.1 above.) The Advance Corporation Tax (ACT) paid by the Company reduced the final Corporation Tax charge, i.e. the 'mainstream corporation tax'. Where the ACT paid exceeded the mainstream corporation tax, the surplus could either (a) be carried forward indefinitely until it can be set off against mainstream corporation tax; or (b) carried back for setting off against unrelieved mainstream corporation tax for the past six years *except* where there had been a change in the ownership of the company. Surplus ACT arising when dividends were paid out of foreign income (FID) could be recovered from the Inland Revenue.

From 6 April 1999, when the imputed tax credit on dividends was reduced to 10%, Advance Corporation Tax ceased to apply. Companies are now required to pay the 10% tax amount within nine months after their year end, and no offset is allowed against their corporation tax liability for the period. Neither the dividends paid nor the 10% imputed tax withheld and passed on to the Inland Revenue can be applied to reduce the profit assessable to corporation tax.

Rates of tax

The rates of corporation tax are:

(a) for small companies, up to 20% in 2000/01 (20% in 1999/00).

From 1 April 2000 there is a new starting rate of 10%. However, this only applies to the first £10 000 of profit and is slowly phased out until profits are £50 000, when the 20% band comes back fully into force.

Where a company has one or more associated companies, the limits are divided by the number of companies involved. A company is associated where one company controls another, or companies are under common control.

Examples:

(i)	Profits	£10 000 @ 10%	= £1 000 payable
(ii)	Profits	£50 000 @ 20%	= £10 000 payable
(iii)	Profits	£20 000	
		– first £10 000 @ 10%	= £1 000
		– second £10,000 @ 22.5%	= £2 250
		Total payable	£3 250
		Effective rate	= 16.25%

For reference, the following rates apply to other profits:

Profits of £30 000 have an effective rate of 18.33%
Profits of £40 000 have an effective rate of 19.38%

(b) for large companies, 30% in 2000/01 and 1999/00. Small companies are those with profits (including dividends received plus the tax credit) up to £300 000. Where profits are above this limit and up to £1 500 000, marginal relief applies. The marginal relief consists of the large company rate on the profits, less 1/40 of the amount by which the profits fall short of the upper limit. Thus, if in 1998/99 profits were £500 000 the corporation tax would be:

		£
	30% on £500 000	150 000
Less:	$\frac{1}{40}$ x (1 500 000 – £500 000)	25 000
		125 000

In this case the corporation tax payable of £125 000 represents an effective rate of 26% on the profits.

The basis of assessment

Limited companies are assessed to corporation tax on their taxable profits, less capital allowances, for each accounting period. The taxable profits include profits from all sources, including capital gains but excluding dividends received from other UK companies. Income tax suffered by imputation from dividends received by the company can be set off against any advance corporation tax due. Corporation tax applies to the year beginning 1 April. Payment is due nine months after the end of the accounting period.

Large companies with taxable profits of £1.5 million p.a. or more (around 20,000 in number) moved to paying corporation tax in quarterly instalments for accounting periods ending on or after 1 July 1999. This new system is being brought in over 4 years.

Computation of profit

The general rule is that a computation for corporation tax purposes is based on income tax principles and is made under the appropriate Schedules and Cases as apply to an income tax computation. The whole of the sources of income which falls under the various Schedules and Cases is, however, aggregated so that a single total is arrived at on which corporation tax is payable. The same rules as for income tax decide what income is assessable or not and what charges are allowable or not; but there are certain exceptions as explained below.

Corporation tax is chargeable on all income, however arising. Income from trading overseas is assessed whether actually received or not but overseas taxation is allowed as a deduction against such income. Dividends received from UK companies are not chargeable to corporation tax.

Capital gains (see later section) are treated as part of profits for the purpose of corporation tax and therefore chargeable at the appropriate corporation tax rate.

Yearly interest and other annual payments are deductible for corporation tax purposes and the system of capital allowances applies. Losses may be carried forward. Trading losses may be set off against other income of the same period or of preceding periods. Dividends or other forms of distribution of profit do not constitute charges against income. Gifts to charities and four-year covenants for charities are allowable expenses, but the company must deduct income tax from the payment.

A specimen computation

The profit and loss account for a company for the year ended 31 March 2000 might show the following figures.

	£	£
Trading profit, adjusted for tax		770 000
Interest on government stock received 31.12.99, gross	10 000	
Dividends from UK companies, received 1.5.99, net	7 200	
		17 200
		787 200
Less: Debenture interest paid, on 31.12.99 gross		80 000
		707 200
Less: Dividends paid 1.6.99		36 600
		670 600

Capital gains for the year were £100 000; loss relief brought forward was £50 000; and capital allowances were £50 000.

N.B. There are several associated companies, so no marginal small company relief is due.

The computation for corporation tax was as follows:

Trading profit	770 000
Add: Interest received	10 000
	780 000
Less: Debenture interest	80 000
	700 000
Add: Capital gains	100 000
	800 000

Less: Capital allowances		50 000
		750 000
Less: Loss relief		50 000
		700 000
Mainstream corporation tax at 30%:		210 000
Less: Tax credits		
On dividends paid:	Nil	
On dividends received:		
1/9 x £7 200	800	
		800
Corporation tax payable		£209 200

Groups of companies

A loss incurred by a company which is a member of a group may be set off against the profit made by another member of the group. The test of group membership is ownership of 75% of the ordinary shares. The right to carry forward a tax loss is restricted where a change in the ownership of a company is associated with a change in the nature of its trade. The 1990 Finance Act included provisions for determination of group relief by Inspectors of Taxes when 'pay and file' procedures came into operation in 1993.

Company buying own shares

This facility was provided by the Companies Act 1981, subject to various qualifications. Taxation aspects are somewhat complex but in general have the effect of preventing the payment taking the form of a tax-free dividend. In the case of unquoted trading companies the sales will not be subject to income tax in the shareholders' hands, but may be subject to capital gains tax.

Demerging and disaggregation

The Finance Act 1980 introduced measures to relieve tax chargeable on distributions (normally in the form of shares) when an incorporated business is split up into genuine incorporated divisions. In 1986/87 severe restrictions were placed on the practice of splitting up businesses to avoid VAT. In the 1995 Budget the Customs and Excise were given immediately improved powers to counter VAT avoidance on groups of companies.

Sales of company

Where a company is sold leaving it without the resources to pay outstanding corporation tax, that tax can be collected from the individuals or company which previously controlled the company sold. This applies to contracts for sale on or after 30 November 1993.

'Know how'

'Know how' is industrial information and techniques likely to assist in the manufacture or processing of goods or materials, etc.

- The cost of 'know how' acquired by a person may be written off for tax purposes at 25% on the reducing balance.
- Receipts from the sale of 'know how' are treated, in a continuing business, as a trading receipt.

Pay and file system (up to 30 June 1999)

This involves companies estimating their corporation tax liability and paying the estimated tax within 9 months after the end of the accounting period. Interest is chargeable on corporation tax which is paid late, and payable on overpaid corporation tax from the later of the due date and the date of payment. Accounts, tax computations and a Return are sent to the appropriate Tax Inspector by 12 months after the end of the accounting period. The system avoids appeals against estimated assessments.

Self-assessment for companies (from 1 July 1999)

This was introduced for accounting periods ending on or after 1 July 1999. This is a relatively small step from Pay-and-File. Unless the Inland Revenue makes an enquiry into the return within 12 months of the filing date it will 'normally' be regarded as finalised.

4.9 INVESTMENT COMPANIES AND CLOSE COMPANIES

General

An investment company is one of which the main purpose is to make and obtain income from investments. These include companies formed for the purpose of administering family investments in securities and land; but there are many large investment companies. The taxable profits of these companies (as well as those of insurance companies) are assessed after deducting 'management expenses' (s 75 Taxes Act 1988), which are essentially the expenses of managing the company as such.

Excess management expenses and charges (such as interest payments) cannot be claimed where, during a three-year period, the ownership of an investment company changes, the business has become small or negligible and is revived after the change, or there is a significant increase in capital three years after the change or before the change (Budget 1994).

Close companies

For accounting periods after 31 March 1989, the legislation covering close companies is confined to close investment companies (CICs). After that date the Finance Act 1989 abolished the previous provisions applied to those close companies of which the purpose was to trade, to let land (other than to persons connected with the company) and to hold shares in an exempt company.

The general purpose of the legislation was to prevent shareholders avoid higher rates of taxation by restricting dividends, or other forms of distribution of profits. If a proportion of profit (generally 70%) was retained in the company the shareholders could be assessed to tax on the profits retained, although substantial reliefs from the apportionment of profits applied to trading close companies.

A close company (i.e. now a close investment company) is one which does not have a quotation on a stock exchange and of which less than 35% of the shares are held by the public. More specifically it is one controlled by five or fewer 'participators' and their associates, of which all partners and near relatives are treated as one individual for the purpose. For 1989/90 onwards close investment companies are liable for corporation tax at 40% on 70% of undistributed profits. The small companies' rate does not apply to these companies.

In some cases a close company makes a loan to an individual so that the latter can acquire convertible loan stock in a company. Interest on the loan gives relief of tax to the individual until the convertible loan stock is converted to ordinary share capital, on the grounds that at that point the individual has obtained value for the assignment of a debt due to him from the company (ICTA 1988 Sections 360 and 363).

A close company making a loan to a participator is liable to tax on the amount of the loan, within 14 days after the end of the accounting period. This provision extends to directors' overdrawn current accounts. This provision has proved to be virtually impossible to operate as very few companies are set up to establish such figures within 14 days of the year end. Accordingly, in the 1995 Budget this period was extended to 9 months for accounting periods ending on or after 31 March 1996. In addition, no tax is to be paid if the 'loan' is repaid within this 9 months. It it is repaid after this 9-month period the tax is paid a year later.

4.10 BUSINESS EXPANSION SCHEME

General

In essence the regulations gave relief of income tax to individuals for investment in the ordinary shares of new companies carrying on new trades or intending to do so within four months of the issue of the shares. The relief consisted of the amount invested in the shares but was reduced by any amount received on the shares, e.g. by way of repayment or sale, within five years of their issue. This relief was particularly valuable to someone paying higher rate tax. The scheme was terminated at the end of December 1993 and was replaced by the Enterprise Investment scheme – see Section **3.7**.

4.11 SELF-EMPLOYED PERSONS

A. Schedule D or Schedule E?

The rules of Schedule E basically apply to persons who work for wages or salaries under a contract of employment. Schedule D, Cases I and II, applies to persons or partners operating a separate business. Apart from remuneration, the advantages of being employed under a contract of service include possible inclusion in the employer's pension scheme, redundancy pay, maternity pay and other business and social security benefits. On the other hand a person operating his or her own business receives more tax allowances for business expenses, but has to pay for pensions, and must, of course, provide capital and accept risk.

Some pressure is exerted by the Inland Revenue to assess under Schedule E rather than Schedule D. Reclassification from Schedule D to Schedule E has applied in particular cases; for example, to club musicians, broadcasting and film technicians, and part-time lecturing. Appeals should be made against unjust classifications but such appeals are unlikely to be successful where there is in fact a relationship of employer and employee.

However, Schedule D is appropriate for a business, even conducted part time, which provides goods and services to a number of customers. The important case of Hall v Lorimer (1992) decided, on appeal, that a freelance vision mixer who carried out over 200 assignments for up to 50 companies was to be assessed under Schedule D.

The tax situation for various occupations is examined below.

B. Authors, artists and entertainers

Authors, artists and entertainers, conducting a business on their own account and not employed at a salary, are assessed under Schedule D, Case II. This means that they can charge against their income the expenses wholly and exclusively incurred in earning that income. The expenses would include: stationery, postage, materials used in the activity, the wardrobe of an actor, and the costs of a study or studio, such as heating, cleaning, rates and rent. If the work is done at home, a proportion of the actual outgoings associated with the accommodation may be charged. Income from royalties or from an outright sale of the work is assessable and must be included in the return, but a lump sum received on sale of the residual rights of a work can be spread forward up to six years, provided the work has been published for 10 years.

In the case of artists who have been engaged on a single work of art for over 12 months, the receipts obtained from such work can be spread for income tax purposes over the period during which it was made.

From 1969 tax cannot be avoided by selling future earnings for a capital sum, this having become a fairly common practice in the theatrical profession.

From 1987/88 non-resident entertainers and sportsmen have had a withholding tax at the basic rate deducted from their UK earnings of at least £500.

Where a theatrical artist works under a contract of employment his or her remuneration is chargeable to tax under Schedule E, for which the deductible expenses are very limited. However, from 1990/91 the employed entertainer can deduct from his or her remuneration the fees paid to an agent who carries on an employment agency under licence. The fees deductible are limited to 17.5% of the emoluments. These provisions apply to a person who is employed as an actor, singer, musician, dancer or theatrical artist.

C. Divers

From 1978/79 the income of divers and diving supervisors operating in the UK or the continental shelf is chargeable under Schedule D Case I, i.e. as a business, and not under Schedule E, as an employment.

D. Farmers

(i) General. Subject to certain special arrangements noted below, farming is assessable to tax as a business under Schedule D, Case I. Assuming the farm is not operated as a limited company, losses incurred by individual farmers can be set off against other income, provided the farm is conducted with a view to profit. No set-off against other income is available to 'hobby farmers' (i.e. those operating without the expectation of profit) and not normally if losses have been incurred after 6 years. Hobby farmers can, however, claim for losses to be carried forward to be set off against any future profits. They may also claim relief against other income for the agricultural use of a farmhouse to the extent that this expenditure cannot be set off against farming income.

(ii) Averaging profits. After 1977/78 individual farmers and partnerships of farmers (not companies) have averaged profits over two consecutive years of assessment, where there is a difference of at least 30% in the profits of these years, with marginal relief for a difference between 25% and 30%.

(iii) Grants. Grants and other government subsidies are included in taxable profits if they represent revenue, not capital receipts.

(iv) Farmhouse. Only the expenses incurred in the business use of the farmhouse is allowed in computing farm profits for tax purposes.

(v) Herd basis. The 'herd' basis of assessment means that by an election within 2 years after the first year of assessment, production herds are treated as capital expenditure, not as stock in trade. Production herds are those intended for obtaining from them product for sale, such as wool and milk, but not livestock for resale in the normal course. Rearing costs and additions, but not replacements to the herd, are also capitalised and do not enter into the tax assessment, nor does the sale of the livestock. Sale of the products of the herd are, however, taxable.

(vi) VAT. Farmers are not required to register for VAT but may apply a fixed rate to sales of produce and this addition is recoverable by a VAT-registered customer.

(vii) Woodlands. The taxation of income from woodlands was abolished in 1988-89. However, for 1995/96 profit on short rotation coppice will be taxed as farming. This is where fast-growing trees are regularly harvested for fuel.

E. Ministers of religion

Ministers of religion may claim a deduction from income for expenses wholly, exclusively and necessarily incurred in carrying out their duties, e.g. motor and travelling expenses so incurred, postage, stationery, the replacement of robes, out-of-pocket payments to curates and lay workers, telephone charges, communion expenses, etc. A minister who pays the rent of his or her private residence may claim a deduction for whatever proportion of that residence is used in connection with his or her duties up to a maximum of one-quarter. A claim can also be made for lighting, heating, and so on, according to the proportion attributable to professional purposes. A case in 1986 decided that a vicar was not entitled to claim capital allowances for a slide projector, because he did not have to incur the expenditure for his work. However a vicar can claim capital allowance on his or her car and office furniture and equipment.

F. Cessation provisions

Certain self-employed professional persons, notably barristers, were until recently taxed on a 'cash basis' – that is, their tax computations cover only actual cash received and paid and do not include amounts due but unpaid. This practice meant that when they ceased to follow their profession, or retired, fees received in cash after cessation escaped tax.

The 1998 Finance Act revoked this privileged treatment of some professionals. It effectively means that those firms who had received authorisation to operate the 'cash basis' will have to include work-in-progress as defined by SSAP 9. Where time ledgers record staff time,then a useful starting point can be using the the proportion of the charge-out rate covering salaries and overhead recovery. Partners' work in progress would normally only include overhead allocation.

The main points of the legislation are as follows:

1. The accounts must be prepared to show a true and fair view of the profits.
2. The first year affected by these provisions is 1999/00.
3. The catch-up charge is payable over 10 years, starting with 1999/00, and there is a capping to restrict the additional charge to one tenth of the total amount or 10% of the normal profits of the business.
4. There is relief for any double charging when the firm first moved from an earnings basis for the first 7 years of practice.

The following points should also be noted:

a. Whilst the charge will be under Schedule D Case VI for the catch-up charge and therefore not liable to Class 4 NIC, losses could be offset against the charge and it will still count as net relevant earnings for pension purposes. It will not be possible to offset overlap relief against the catch-up charge. The taxpayer will be able to opt to pay the whole catch-up charge at once but unless told to the contrary the 10-year spreading provisions would apply. Also, it should be noted that where a sole practitioner ceases to practice, the 10-year spread will continue but this will be on a fixed one tenth of the charge basis.
b. Partnerships – where w new partner joins the firm, it will be spread between the partners for the year in which the deferred charge bites in the profit sharing ration of that year. It is important to note that incoming partners will be buying into the deferred catch-up charge.

G. Subcontractors in construction industry

From 5 April 1972, remuneration paid to subcontractors in the construction industry in the UK or offshore is subject to deduction of income tax at the basic rate. The amount deducted is treated as a payment on account of the subcontractor's tax liabilities for the year. The 'construction industry' in this context covers a wide field of work connected with buildings, and includes not only the actual construction but also, for instance, decorating, repairs, plumbing, heating installation and electrical work.

The regulations do not apply to the wages or salaries of employees of the contractor, because employees' wages continue to be subject to deductions of tax under the PAYE system. A certificate of exemption (known as a 714) from these provisions may be obtained from the Inspector of Taxes if he is satisfied that appropriate accounts are being kept; the applicant has adequate premises and facilities; and that there is at least three years' proper compliance with the obligations under the Tax Acts and other relevant legal requirements. Special exemption certificates are obtainable by school and college leavers, and certain others, under guarantee.

However, from 1 August 1999, virtually all of these certificates are to be withdrawn. Only those with high turnovers, i.e. a history of £30 000 plus p.a. excluding direct costs such as materials, and paid by bank transfer will be eligible. Others will need to obtain a registration card to allow contractors to pay them at all. A sum will still be deducted at the current penal rate of 23%. Previously it was thought that it would be a lower rate to take account of personal allowances and expenses.

Over the past few years many people in the construction industry have been treated as subcontractors even though they work for only one organisation year in year out. Until 1996 the Inland Revenue turned a blind eye to what was effectively an employer-employee relationship. Tax was after all being collected either at source, or by reputable tax payers filing accounts on time at the threat of losing their 714 certificates. However, National Insurance at the much higher Class 1 (employer) rates were being lost. Most permanent subcontractors lost their self-employed status within the first few months of 1997. Also those subcontractors 'employed' via agencies also fell within the net from April 1998. For further details see Inland Revenue leaflet 148 'Are your workers employed or self-employed?'.

CHAPTER 5

CAPITAL GAINS

5.1 GENERAL NATURE OF THE TAX

Capital gains and capital losses refer to profits or losses on the sale or disposal otherwise of assets, including land and buildings, shares and securities, etc.; this does not include business stock held for sale, which is taxed through the normal process of taxing business profits. In essence a gain occurs when an asset is sold for more than it cost, and a loss is the reverse, but there are many qualifications to this simple statement, as will appear below. For sales after 5 April 1988 of assets held at 31 March 1982 the value at the latter date is normally substituted for the cost.

The tax applies to persons who are resident and ordinarily resident in the UK on gains arising both in the UK and abroad. Up to 6 April 1990 the gains of husband and wife were aggregated except where separate assessments were claimed, but since that date each party is assessed separately. Individuals do not pay tax on the first £7 200 in 2000/01 and £7 100 in 1999/00. There are many other exemptions (see below). Most trusts are exempt to half the usual rate. Full exemption will, however, apply to trusts for the mentally handicapped, persons receiving attendance allowance, and the middle or higher range of disability allowance.

5.2 RATES OF TAX

Limited companies

Both small and large companies bear corporation tax on their capital gains at the appropriate corporation tax rates.

Investment trusts, unit trusts and funds in court

The 1980 Finance Act gave these bodies complete exemption from capital gains. Investors are liable for capital gains tax on the realisation of their interests in the trusts.

Individuals

Individuals were liable to capital gains tax at their marginal rate of income tax – in 1998/99 and 1997/98 at 20%, 23% or 40%. For 1999/00 even though the Income Tax band of 20% had been abolished, capital gains will be taxed at 20% or 40% (the new 10% band for income tax did not count.) From 6 April 2000, the 10% band does count.

Discretionary accumulation and maintenance trusts

From 1996/97 onwards, capital gains tax is payable at 34% (previously the basic rate of income tax plus 10%), including, from 6 April 1998, all gains realised by trustees and by personal representatives of deceased persons (previously 23%).

5.3 THE PRINCIPAL EXCEPTIONS

The following gains are not chargeable to the tax:

- The principal residence of an individual or a house which he or she owns and occupies or which is occupied rent free by a dependent relative before 6 April 1988, or where a person is required by the terms of his employment to live in other accommodation. See below for further comment.
- Vehicles of the private car type not used for business.
- Goods and chattels sold for no more than £6 000. For a sale price above these limits the gain is limited to 5/3rds of the excess.
- Certain forms of savings, such as: National Savings Certificates, National Development Bonds, Defence Bonds, Save As You Earn and TESSA bonuses, ISA gains and Premium Bonds.
- Sums received on the maturity or surrender of life assurance policies by the original owner, or where they are gifts to the taxpayer.
- Moveable property with predictable life of under 50 years, e.g. wasting assets, such as animals and boats, not subject to capital allowances. Special provisions apply to leases of 50 years or less. Other wasting assets must be written down progressively and only the balance of cost can be set against sale proceeds for capital gains purposes.
- The first £7 200 of capital gains in 2000/01 and £7 100 in 1999/00. From 5 April 1990 both husband and wife obtain this exemption.
- Gains on the disposal of British government securities and those guaranteed by the British government; and corporate bonds, debentures and loan stock, if the company has a quotation on a stock exchange, but not loans convertible into shares, unmarketable securities, those carrying excessive interest and those linked to a share index.
- Gifts to charities and the capital gains of charities.
- Gifts or sales by a taxpayer to his or her spouse, but in this case the spouse will be assumed to have acquired the asset at the date and cost when it was originally acquired.
- From 13 March 1989 gifts of certain business assets are available for hold over relief – see below under 'Gifts'.
- The first £3 600 of gains for trusts in 2000/01 (£3 550 in 1999/00), or £7 200 (£7 100 in 1999/00) for trusts for the mentally handicapped and

those receiving the middle or higher rate of disability living allowance.

- The first holder of Business Expansion Scheme shares issued after 18 March 1986, and the first disposal of shares under the Enterprise Investment Scheme.
- Capital gains in personal equity plans.
- Capital gains which relate to the period before 1 April 1982.
- Transfers between husband and wife.

5.4 CALCULATING THE GAIN (INCLUDING INDEXATION)

The general method

A capital gain or loss is essentially the difference between the cost of an asset and the proceeds of sale, subject to 'rebasing' – see below. The costs include the incidental expenses incurred on acquisition or disposal, e.g. professional fees, commission and stamp duty. From the resultant gain an indexation allowance is deducted to offset inflation since 31 March 1982, or the date of acquisition, if later. The legislation is complex and special rules apply to part disposals of investments, disposals and acquisitions of investments in the same period of stock exchange account, investments pooled for tax purposes, transfers between company groups and disposals in company reorganisations and reconstructions.The March 1998 budget abolished the indexation allowance (not for companies) with effect from 6 April 1998. However, for an asset held before that date an allowance for indexation will be available up to 5 April 1998.

From 6 April 1998 onwards Tapering Relief will be available (see below).

Rebasing

Rebasing applies to assets held at 31 March 1982 and means that the value of the assets at that date is normally substituted for their cost in calculating a gain or loss. Subject to the following qualifications all disposals of these assets are rebased for disposals after 5 April 1988; previously the taxpayer had an option to do so.

It will be assumed that no loss or gain arises in the following circumstances:

- Where a gain arises on rebasing but a smaller gain or a loss would have arisen without rebasing, i.e. if the actual cost of an asset acquired before 31 March 1982 was set off against the sales proceeds.
- Where a loss arises on rebasing but either a smaller loss or a gain would have arisen without rebasing.

The foregoing assumptions will not apply if an election (irrevocable) is made for all assets (including those acquired before 6 April 1965) held at 31 March 1988 to be rebased, but only in special circumstances will such an election be beneficial. Unless rebased to 31 March 1982 the cost of assets held at 6 April 1965 was taken to be their value at that date, subject to a time apportionment for assets other than securities and development land, and subject to indexation from 31 March 1982. The value of assets at 6 April 1965 will, however, rarely be greater than their value at 31 March 1982.

Indexation

Gains after 31 March 1982 are reduced by applying to the cost the rise in the Retail Price Index since acquisition up to 5 April 1998, if the asset is disposed of after this date. The taxpayer may apply for indexation to be applied to the value of the asset rather than to the original cost. From 30 November 1993 indexation cannot be used to create or augment a loss. From 4 July 1987 indexation cannot be applied to shares in building societies or industrial and provident societies.

An example of indexation

The following example shows the calculation of the gain in a simple case where the asset was acquired in March 1987 and sold in October 1998. The indexation allowances for assets disposed of in April 1998 are shown below. These indices will change in subsequent months.

	£	£
Price received on sale	65 000	
Less: Incidental expenses on sale	2 000	
Net proceeds on sale		63 000
Price paid on acquisition	29 000	
Add: Incidental expenses on purchase	1 000	
Total cost of acquisition		30 000
Gain before indexation		33 000
Less: Indexation allowance		
£30 000 x 0.580 $\frac{(164.5 - 104.1)}{104.1}$		17 406
NET GAIN		£15 594

Note that this particular gain is above the individual's exemption limit but would be added to other gains, less losses, for the tax year, and the exemption limit would be deducted from the total.

Capital Gains Tax Indexation Allowance

The gains arising on the disposal of an asset may be reduced by an indexation allowance which is calculated by reference to increases in the Retail Prices Index published by the Department of Employment. The allowance is available from 6 April 1981 (1 April 1981 for companies).The Index was published until January 1987 using an average of 100 for January 1974 as a basis, and after January 1987 using and average of 100 for January 1987 as a basis. The Retail Price Index figures published are set out below.

For individuals, indexation ceased for assets acquire post 6 April 1998 and replaced by taper relief (see Section 5.5 below). For other assets held before then, indexation will be allowed from the date of acquisition to April 1998 and taper relief thereafter. There is *no* change for taxpayers liable to corporation tax.

Prices at January 1974 = 100

Year	Jan	Feb	Mar	Apr	May	Jun	Jul	Aug	Sep	Oct	Nov	Dec
1982			313.4	319.7	322.0	322.9	323.0	323.1	322.9	324.5	326.1	325.5
1983	325.9	327.3	327.9	332.5	333.9	334.7	336.5	338.0	339.5	340.7	341.9	342.8
1984	342.6	344.0	345.1	349.7	351.0	351.9	351.5	354.8	355.5	357.7	358.8	358.5
1985	359.8	362.7	366.1	373.9	375.6	376.4	375.7	376.7	376.5	377.1	378.4	378.9
1986	379.7	378.1	386.1	385.3	386.0	385.8	384.7	385.9	387.8	388.4	391.7	393.0
1987	394.5											

Prices at January 1987 = 100

Year	Jan	Feb	Mar	Apr	May	Jun	Jul	Aug	Sep	Oct	Nov	Dec
1987	100.0	100.4	100.6	101.8	101.9	101.9	101.8	102.1	102.4	102.9	103.4	103.3
1988	103.3	103.7	104.1	105.8	106.2	106.6	106.7	107.9	108.4	109.5	110.0	110.3
1989	111.0	111.8	112.3	114.3	115.0	115.4	115.5	115.8	116.6	117.5	118.3	118.8
1990	119.5	120.2	121.4	125.1	126.2	126.7	126.8	128.1	129.3	130.3	130.0	129.9
1991	130.2	130.9	131.4	133.1	133.5	134.1	133.8	134.1	134.6	135.1	135.6	135.7
1992	135.6	136.3	136.7	138.8	139.3	139.3	138.8	138.9	139.4	139.9	139.7	139.2
1993	137.9	138.8	139.3	140.6	141.1	141.0	140.7	141.3	141.9	141.8	141.6	141.9
1994	141.3	142.1	142.5	144.2	144.7	144.7	144.0	144.7	145.0	145.2	145.3	146.0
1995	146.0	146.9	147.5	149.0	149.6	149.8	149.1	149.9	150.6	149.8	149.8	150.7
1996	150.2	150.9	151.5	152.6	152.9	153.0	152.4	153.1	153.8	153.8	153.9	154.4
1997	154.4	155.0	155.4	156.3	156.9	157.5	157.5	158.5	159.3	159.5	159.6	160.0
1998	159.5	160.3	160.8	162.6	163.5	163.4	163.0	163.7	164.4	164.5	164.4	164.4
1999	163.4	163.7	164.1	165.2	165.6	165.6	165.1	165.5	166.2	166.5	166.7	167.3
2000	166.6	167.5										

Using RI as the Retail Price Index for March 1982 if the asset was acquired prior to April 1981, or the month falling 12 months after the date on which the asset was acquired or expenditure incurred, and RD as the Retail Price Index for the month in which the disposal was made (or April 1998 if later and an individual), the indexation allowance is calculated by the formula:

$$\frac{RD - RI}{RI}$$ rounded to the nearest third decimal place.

5.5 TAPERING RELIEF (NOT FOR LIMITED COMPANIES)

From 6 April 1998, taper relief is available generally but is biased in favour of 'business assets'. The taper reduces the chargeable gain according to how long (complete periods of 12 months) the asset has been held. Only complete holding years which start after 5 April 1998 count. Where an asset was held before 17 March 1998 (budget day) one bonus year will be added to the actual number of complete post-5 April 1998 years.

For example an asset acquired on 1 March 1998 and disposed of on 1 February 2001 will have been held for two years and almost ten months after 5 April 1998 – i.e. only two complete years – but transitionally the holding period will be taken as three years.

(a) Year 2000/01. The March budget announced substantial changes to the CGT business taper relief rules. The period for which the relevant business assets have to be held to secure the 10% rate of tax has been reduced from 10 years to 4 years. A higher rate CGT payer will only have to pay an effective 35% rate of tax on the gain arising on the disposal of relevant assets held more than one year but less than two, 30% for assets held more than two years but less than three, 20% for assets held more than three years but less than four and 10% for assets held for more than four years.

For relevant assets held at 17 March 1998, the rate of tax applying to a gain on a disposal in the tax year ended 5 April 2001 will be 30%. For disposals in the year ended 5 April 2002, the tax rate on the gain will be 20%. For disposals after 5 April 2002, the tax rate will be 10%

For non-business assets, the existing ten-year non-business rate of taper relief, together with the additional year for assets held at 17 March 1998, will continue to apply.

The previous limits for shareholdings in unquoted and quoted trading companies will also be substantially reduced.

The following shareholdings will qualify as business assets:

- All shareholdings held by employees and others in unquoted trading companies.
- All shareholdings held by employees in quoted trading companies.
- Shareholdings in a quoted trading company where the holder is not an employee but can exercise at least 5% of the voting rights.

Shares traded in the Alternative Investment Market of the London Stock Exchange will be treated as unquoted.

Where shares qualify as a business asset only from that date, an apportionment of the eventual gain will be necessary so that part qualifies as business rate of taper and the balance for non-business taper.

Number of complete years after 5/4/98 for which asset held	% of gain chargeable		Equivalent tax rates for 40% and 20% rate taxpayer	
	business assets	non-business assets	business assets	non-business assets
0	100	100	40/20.0	40/20.0
1	87.5	100	37/17.5	40/20.0
2	75.0	100	34/15.0	40/20.0
3	50.0	95	31/10.0	38/19.0
4	25.0	90	28/5.0	36/18.0
5	25.0	85	25/5.0	34/17.0
6	25.0	80	22/5.0	32/16.0
7	25.0	75	19/5.0	30/15.0
8	25.0	70	13/5.0	28/14.0
9	25.0	65	13/5.0	26/13.0
10 or more	25.0	60	10/5.0	24/12.0

(b) For the years ending 5 April 2000, business assets, ten or more holding years attracted 75% relief (i.e. only 25% of the gain is chargeable – equivalent to reducing a 40% rate of capital gain to 10%). Pro-rata relief is given for shorter periods – 7.5% for one complete year, 15% for two, etc. 'Business assets' are broadly those used for the individual's trade, partnership trade, or full-time office or employment, or in a qualifying company in which the owner must have specified voting rights.

For non-business assets, there is a minimum holding period of three complete years; 5% is then given, 10% after 4 years, etc. up to 40% relief after 10 or more years – equivalent to reducing a 40% capital gain to 24%.

As a consequence pooling of identical securities will cease from 6 April 1998, so that individual purchases can be identified.

Number of complete years after 5/4/98 for which asset held	% of gain chargeable		Equivalent tax rates for 40% and 20% rate taxpayer	
	business assets	non-business assets	business assets	non-business assets
0	100	100	40/20.0	40/20.0
1	92.5	100	37/18.5	40/20.0
2	85	100	34/17.0	40/20.0
3	77.5	95	31/15.5	38/19.0
4	70	90	28/14.0	36/18.0
5	62.5	85	25/12.5	34/17.0
6	55	80	22/11.0	32/16.0
7	47.5	75	19/9.5	30/15.0
8	40	70	13/6.5	28/14.0
9	32.5	65	13/6.5	26/13.0
10	25	60	10/5.0	24/12.0

5.6 TRUSTEES

Trustees are liable for capital gains on the sale of trust assets, at the income tax rate, but the beneficiaries under the trust will not be liable for the tax when they dispose of their interests under the trust. This provision has the effect of avoiding a double charge on the persons ultimately entitled to the benefit of the assets held in trust for them. (See also **5.10** Death of the Taxpayer.)

The beneficiary of an overseas trust is liable to pay capital gains tax on remittances to him or her of the trust's gains. There is no exemption from the tax when an interest in an overseas trust is disposed of. Measures to prevent tax avoidance by setting up overseas trusts were introduced in 1991/92.

5.7 LOSSES

Losses on the sale of assets can be set off against capital gains and any losses not used in this way can be carried forward. The loss concerned is the loss referable to the period after 31 March 1982 calculated in the manner indicated in section 5.4 above. For 1977/78 and onwards losses brought forward will be used only to the extent necessary to reduce gains to the exemption limit.

Losses incurred by individuals on the disposal of shares taken up in unquoted trading companies may be set off against income for income tax purposes; balances unrelieved in this way can be set off against capital gains.

Relief of capital gains tax applies to losses incurred from irrecoverable loans and payments under guarantees granted to borrowers for trading purposes. This relief is not applicable to loans between members of a group of companies.

5.8 SALE OF BUSINESS ON RETIREMENT

Up to 5 April 1999, exemption from capital gains tax on gains of up to £250 000 is available where a taxpayer aged 55 (aged 50 from 28 November 1995) sells a business he or she has owned for 10 years. Half of the next £750 000 is also exempt. Consecutive periods of ownership by either husband or wife may be aggregated. The relief also applies to the sale of shares in a family company. Where ownership is less than 10 years 10% of the relief is available for one year, 20% for two years, and so on. On and after 16 March 1993 the shareholding condition is reduced to a single individual 5% test. If a taxpayer retires before the above age on grounds of ill-health then there is relief available – subject to certain conditions.

However, from 6 April 1999 this relief is phased out over 5 years by a gradual reduction of the above relief limits. The limits will reduce by 1/5 each year (from 6 April 1999) so that no relief will be available in

2003/04. The computational rules will remain the same in all other respects.

During the phasing out, the relief will continue to be given against qualifying chargeable gains after indexation allowance but before taper relief. The taxpayer will be able to allocate retirement relief against different gains such as to maximise taper relief.

5.9 REPLACEMENT OF ASSETS (ROLLOVER RELIEF)

This relief enables the payment of capital gains tax to be postponed, possibly indefinitely, when a business asset is sold and is replaced by another asset. It applies to land and buildings, fixed plant, ships and aircraft, property let commercially and let as furnished holiday accommodation, and goodwill, and it is not necessary that the new asset is of the same kind as the old asset. It does not apply to movable plant or machinery, farming, property development, or where half a company's assets are held in land, or motor cars.

In the case of the sale of a non-depreciating asset, e.g. land and buildings, the capital gain is set off against the cost of the new asset and thus is not payable until the new asset is sold. However, a gain on the sale of a new asset could again be rolled over by a further replacement and so on indefinitely. Rollover relief is available to landlords selling land or buildings to tenants who have rights to acquire the freehold reversions under the Leasehold Reform Act 1967 and the Housing and Urban Development Act 1993, provided reinvestment is made in replacement land and buildings.

Where a depreciating asset is sold the capital gain is not deducted from the cost of a replacement but is postponed for 10 years unless meanwhile the new asset has been sold or replaced by a non-depreciating asset. Depreciating assets are those with a predictable life of under 50 years such as boats and animals, and leases with an unexpired term of 60 years.

In all cases the new asset must be acquired not earlier than one year before and not later than three years after the sale of the old asset, but there can be some flexibility in these limits by agreement of the Inspector, in certain circumstances.

If the cost of a new asset is less than the gross proceeds from the sale of the old asset then the difference (if less than the gain) represents the capital gain on which tax must be paid and only the balance of the gain can be rolled over.

On and after 1 January 1993 rollover relief applies to EU quotas for the premium given to producers of ewes and calves and suckler cows, milk and potato quotas being already included since 1987.

From 20 June 1994 the amount of the gains which can be rolled over into a qualifying investment cannot exceed the acquisition cost of the replacement investment. The excess is not ever liable to tax.

Rollover relief applies when one company in a group transfers an asset to another group member at a gain. The relief does not apply to so-called 'roll around' when assets are transferred within a group but no replacement asset is acquired. The relief does apply where land is disposed of by one member of a group as a result of compulsory purchase, and replacement land is acquired by another group member. These provisions were announced in the 1994 Budget but have represented a long-standing practice.

5.10 DEATH OF THE TAXPAYER

No capital gains tax is payable but there may be a liability for inheritance tax (see Chapter 9). The persons who inherit the assets are assumed to take them at their market value at the date of death. This treatment applies to settled property on which the deceased had an interest.

Personal representatives can charge the expenses of establishing title in computing the gains or losses on the sale of assets in a deceased person's estate. Either the actual justifiable expenses can be charged or a scale effective after 5 April 1993 applied. From the same date corporate trustees must apply a further scale of charges for transfers of assets to beneficiaries and for actual disposals and acquisitions (S/P 8/94, 16.9.94).

5.11 PAYMENT OF TAX

Payment is due on 31 January after the end of the tax year in which the gains accrued.

5.12 SALE OF PRIVATE HOUSE

As mentioned in section 5.3 above, capital gains tax is not payable on the sale of the principal private residence owned and occupied by a taxpayer. If the taxpayer owns and occupies more than one private residence he or she should advise the Inspector of Taxes which is to be treated as the principal private residence for exemption purposes. Subject to the qualifications set out below, the taxpayer will be liable for a proportion of the gain on the sale of the principal private residence corresponding to the periods when he or she was not in occupation of that house:

- Exemption applied to a house owned by the taxpayer and occupied rent free by a dependent relative before 6 April 1988.
- Absence due to having to live elsewhere under a contract of employment is ignored, e.g. a vicar who has to live in his or her parish; so is up to four years' total absences due to working away from home; and all absences while working abroad.
- Periods of absence of up to three years in total are ignored, and so are absences in the last three years (1991/92) for the purposes of selling the house.

- Full exemption applies where part of a house is let as residential accommodation, provided the part let does not exceed the part occupied by the taxpayer, with a maximum relief of £40 000 in 1991/92 (previously £20 000).
- Where a taxpayer carries on a business in part of a house exclusively set aside for that purpose, there will be a liability for capital gains tax on that part. The mere use of non-exclusive facilities, even if a charge is claimed in the business assessment, should not, however, give rise to a capital gains assessment.

5.13 HUSBAND AND WIFE

Gains or losses of husband and wife up to 6 April 1990 were aggregated, and the tax payable was the responsibility of the husband, who was entitled to a single annual exemption limit only. With independent taxation of married women after 5 April 1990, the wife is liable for tax on the gains made from the disposal of the assets she owns. She will pay at her marginal rate of income tax, i.e. in 2000/01 10%, 20% and 40% (1999/00 20% and 40%), and will be entitled to her own annual exemption limit of £7 200 in 2000/01 (£7 100 in 1999/00). Where assets are owned jointly by husband and wife, any gain will be shared equally, in the absence of other evidence as to the ownership of shares. By transferring investments and other chargeable assets from one party to the other full advantage can be taken of each party's exemption limits. See **5.17** Bed and Breakfasting.

5.14 GIFTS

A gift from one person to another is a 'disposal' and if the market value of the asset at the time when the gift was made exceeds the cost, the difference is basically a capital gain. To the extent that an asset is transferred at a price below open market value the difference is treated as a gift. No tax is payable by the giver of a chattel when the gift is below the chattels exemption limit of £6 000. Nor would the giver be liable to capital gains tax where his total capital gains in a tax year were within the tax-free limits.

'Hold-over relief' for gifts made before 14 March 1989 had the effect of giving general relief to the giver but this general relief was cancelled on that date. Hold-over relief meant that the recipient of a gift took the asset for tax purposes at the market value less the capital gains made by the giver. The capital gains tax liability was thus deferred until the recipient sold or otherwise disposed of the gifted asset. This relief now applies only to gifts of certain business and other assets to a UK resident. The assets concerned are as follows: assets of a trade, profession, vocation or family company including shares in a family trading company or in unquoted trading companies; agricultural property where the giver has vacant possession; heritage property; charitable gifts and those to political parties (with some qualifications) and housing associations; and capital paid from accumulation and maintenance trusts not later than payments of income.

After 13 March 1989 capital gains tax may be paid by ten equal annual instalments on disposals of land, unquoted shares, and controlling holdings of quoted shares, subject to an election being made. The Inland Revenue Shares Valuation Office will value unquoted shares at 31 March 1982 where all shareholders with similar holdings agree.

5.15 COMPANY LEAVING GROUP

Where a company leaves a group any asset acquired from another group member within the preceding 6 years is a deemed disposal of the asset at the date of acquisition. The chargeable gain or loss accrues immediately before the company left the group. The 1994 Budget contained measures to prevent tax avoidance by artificial degrouping.

5.16 REINVESTMENT IN UNQUOTED COMPANIES

The provisions apply on or after 16 March 1993 to full-time working directors and certain employees owning over 5% of the shares in their unquoted trading companies. The November 1993 Budget extended tax relief for all chargeable gains realised by individuals and trustees, where the beneficiaries of the trust are individuals. Where these shares are sold for reinstatement within 3 years in other companies of a similar nature, capital gains on the sale of the original company's shares are deferred. This means that the capital gains tax liability will not arise until the second company's shares are sold.

5.17 BED AND BREAKFASTING

"Bed and Breakfasting" is a stock market expression describing the practise of selling shares immediately repurchasing them in order to crystalise capital gains (to utilise an annual exemption) or losses (to offset other gains). Typically a sale late on day 1 is followed by a similar purchase early on day 2, when hopefully the price will be much the same.

However, following the 1998 budget, disposals and acquisitions by individuals or trustees of shares of the same class in the same company within a 30-day period are to be matched for capital gain so that no gain or loss is realised.

However, there is currently no prohibition on shares being sold by one spouse on day 1 and "repurchased" by the other spouse on day 2.

CHAPTER 6

RENTS FROM PROPERTY

6.1 GENERAL

In general rent and other income, less allowable expenses, receivable from the letting of land and buildings is assessable to tax. This applies whether the letting is furnished or unfurnished, of a single room, or of a major block of buildings or area of land. The exception is the situation of mutual trading, as where rents are received from its members by a housing association not conducted for profit.

On and after 6 April 1995 all income from property in the UK, whether from furnished or unfurnished letting, is pooled and assessed under Schedule A (Budget 1994). The computation will generally follow the rules applicable to trading profits assessable under Schedule D, using standard accounting principles, but the income is regarded as investment income. Capital allowances continue to apply where applicable, including wear and tear allowances for furnished letting. Losses can be set off against pooled income and unrelieved losses can be carried forward. Income from overseas property will generally follow the above rules but will be assessable under Schedule D, Case V. Corporation tax on let property is unaffected.

6.2 UNFURNISHED AND FURNISHED LETTINGS – SCHEDULE A

Rents received less certain expenses are taxable on a 'current year' basis. Provisional assessments based on the previous year's net income are adjusted subsequently as necessary, when the actual figures for the year are agreed. Payment of the tax is as for Self-Assessment: two payments on account and a balancing payment – the first is paid on 31 January in the tax year, the second on 31st July following the tax year, and the final balancing payment made the next 31 January. The payments on account are 50% (each) of the previous year's liability. Application may be made to reduce these payments if rents are falling, but interest payments may be made if the amount reduced is excessive. The net rents which are chargeable to tax may be those due under a weekly tenancy or even under a lease granted for hundreds of years.

The expenses which may be deducted for tax purposes from the rental income cover: maintenance and repair of the property, services provided, insurance, rates, rent payable, capital allowances or 10% wear and tear allowance on equipment provided and management expenses such as agent's commission for obtaining tenants and for rent collection.

These expenses must have been incurred during the currency of the lease, so that expenses incurred before the landlord under assessment took over the premises cannot be charged. Capital expenditure, such as the cost of extensions and improvements to premises, is disallowed. No capital allowance or depreciation of the property itself is allowable under Schedule A, but capital allowances may be claimed on plant and machinery used for the maintenance and management of the property. If the landlord occupies part of the premises let, the expenses must be apportioned on an equitable basis.

The following is an example of a lettings computation under Schedule A.

	£	£
Rents receivable		20 000
Less: expenses:		
Water rates	3 000	
Maintenance of property	500	
Maintenance of furniture, etc.	250	
Insurance of furnishings	500	
Cleaning and other services	600	
Depreciation of furniture – normally at 10% of rent less water rates = 10% (20 000 - 3 000)	1 700	
		6550
Taxable profit		13 450

Note: If only part of a house was let the total council tax, water rates and other expenses would need apportioning on a reasonable basis, e.g. on floor space.

Where gross rents do not exceed £15 000 it is only necessary to submit to the Inspector of Taxes a statement showing gross income, total expenses and profit.

Losses may be carried forward to be set off against future profits, remembering that from 6 April 1995 all income from property is pooled.

Apportionments of premiums received for leases granted for 50 years or less are treated as rent in the year when the lease was granted. The basis of the calculation is the premium less one fiftieth for each year of the lease after the first year. For example, if a lease is granted for ten years at a premium of £2 000, the following amount is to be added to the rent in the first year:

Premium	£2 000
Less $\frac{10 - 1}{50}$ x £2 000	360
	£1 640

A premium will be assumed where the tenant agrees to carry out work, or to make a payment in lieu of rent or as consideration for the surrender of the lease.

Business rents and connected persons. 'Connected persons' mean generally close relatives of individuals, and companies under common control. Where rent, such as for business premises, is paid between connected persons, it will, after 10 March 1992, be assessed on the recipient as it accrues, not when it is actually received. This applies to rent payable in arrears and when it is an allowable expense for business purposes. The object of the rule is to prevent deferment of tax by the recipient of the accruing income.

Short lets. It is not always appreciated that returns must be made to the Inspector of Taxes of profits from the occasional letting of rooms and that these profits are liable to tax. The consequence of a failure to make returns may be an estimated assessment going back many years, interest and possible penalties. (But see 6.4 below, Rent a Room Scheme.)

6.3 FURNISHED HOLIDAY LETTINGS

The letting of furnished holiday accommodation is basically taxed in the same way as other furnished lettings. However, letting of holiday accommodation 'on a commercial basis' can be treated in 1982/83 and onwards as a trade in accordance with the rules of Schedule D, Case I, with consequent tax advantages.

For the letting to be treated as a trade the holiday accommodation must be available to the public generally for at least 140 days in a year, must in fact be let for a total of 70 days, and must not be in the same occupation for a continuous period of more than 31 days. These periods can be averaged where a number of lettings in different premises are made.

As for other furnished lettings, the assessment is on the current year's profits and tax is payable in two instalments on 1 January in the year of assessment and the following 1 July. A loss can be carried forward or carried back for three years. Capital allowances may be claimed. Note that the rents may be subject to VAT if they exceed £52 000 from 1 April 2000.

Hold-over relief for capital gains is available on disposal of the property.

The letting of caravans on a commercial basis is also normally assessable under the rules of Schedule D.

6.4 RENT A ROOM SCHEME

A relief was introduced from 1992/93 for individuals – owner occupiers and tenants – who let furnished accommodation in their only or main home.

Gross annual rents from this letting which do not exceed £4 250 in 1997/98 to 1999/00 will be exempt from income tax altogether. Where the income exceeds £4 250 the person receiving the rent can either:

- pay tax on the amount by which the gross rent exceeds £4 250, without any further tax deduction for expenses, or
- pay tax on the profit (gross rents less actual expenses) in the normal way.

Where the rent is received jointly, such as in the case of a married couple sharing the income or by other than the resident, the limit of £4 250 is reduced by half to £2 125.

See Inland Revenue leaflet 'Rooms to let' (IR 87).

CHAPTER 7

MISCELLANEOUS MATTERS

7.1 ADDITIONAL ASSESSMENTS

Where the Inspector of Taxes discovers that there has been an undercharge to tax, the Revenue has the authority to make an additional assessment at any time up to six years from the end of the tax year concerned.

If, however, there has been fraud or negligent conduct on the part of the taxpayer or a person acting on his or her behalf, the six-year limit is inoperative and additional assessments can be made for more than six years. A uniform time limit of 20 years applies for the recovery of tax in the case of default. But for whatever reason the income was not brought into charge earlier, assessments of this kind relating to income arising before the date of death cannot be made on the executors or administrators of a deceased person after the end of the third year following the year of assessment in which the person died.

Where the taxpayer has acted fraudulently, the Revenue authorities are permitted to impose penalties of varying sums as well as such additional assessments as may be appropriate. From 5 April 1988 failure to notify liability to tax can involve a penalty up to the amount of tax unpaid. In some instances the mitigation of penalties is allowed and, where that is so, the individual is invariably dealt with more leniently when he has voluntarily made a full and complete disclosure of the facts before their discovery by the Inspector. Penalty negotiations, particularly where large sums are involved, need to be handled with extreme care, and the assistance of an adviser well experienced in these negotiations is recommended.

Part or all of the undercharge is remitted where it is due to an error by the tax authorities and the taxpayer believed that his affairs were in order. In these circumstances the additional assessment must be made within 12 months after the tax year concerned (Finance Act 1989).

7.2 CLUBS AND SOCIETIES

Many clubs, societies and other unincorporated associations are formed for the mutual benefit of the members and to provide communal services. These associations are generally considered to be 'companies' for taxation purposes and are therefore basically liable to corporation tax on trading, investment and letting income, as well as capital gains. Approved charitable associations are exempt, however, from tax. From 1 April 1986 many supplies used by charities are zero-rated for VAT.

The subscriptions and contributions payable by members are not normally taxable, nor are payments made by club members for goods and facilities which the club is set up to provide for them. On the basis that members' subscriptions and other receipts are applied to meet the running expenses of the club, they are not chargeable for the purpose of calculating the profit assessable for corporation tax.

Corporation tax will, however, be payable on the following:

- Activities which constitute trading, such as the holding of sales, sporting events, displays and the letting of club facilities for private purposes, and in these cases the applicable expenses can be set off against the income. However, tax will not normally be charged where the club makes it known that the profits from a particular event will be donated to charity and there is no regular trading or competition with other traders.
- Interest received, such as from bank deposits or from government or local authority stock, and including interest on national savings, but not dividends from UK companies. Where income tax is deducted from the interest, it can be set off against any corporation tax payable by the club, but the interest gross of income tax is chargeable in the corporation tax assessment. Building society interest must be grossed up for income tax by adding ¼ to the amount received and the income tax is likewise deductible from the gross corporation tax. Note that dividends received from UK companies are not chargeable to corporation tax and the tax 'imputed' to the dividend cannot be reclaimed.

Because the assessable profits of a club are likely to be small, i.e. below £300 000, they will probably pay corporation tax at the lower rate, or even from 1 April 2000 the introductory rate of 10%. In any event, provided they do not carry out competitive trading but apply surpluses to charities or club purposes, they should be able to avoid paying corporation tax, except on interest receivable.

7.3 THE COUNCIL TAX

The nature of the tax

The former Community Charge was replaced by the Council Tax from 1 April 1993. Half the council tax consists of a personal element based on the residents in a dwelling, subject to the number of exceptions and reliefs; the other half is a property element based on the value of the property, also subject to exemptions. Dwellings were valued at their saleable value on 1 April 1991 but there is provision for appeals against the valuations if made before the beginning of the council tax year. The valuations were placed in bands as follows:

Band	*Values*
A	up to £40,000
B	£ 40,001 to 52,000
C	£ 52,001 to 68,000
D	£ 68,001 to 88,000
E	£ 88,001 to 120,000
F	£120,001 to 160,000
G	£160,001 to 320,000
H	above £320,000

Exempt dwellings

Dwellings exempt from tax are those exclusively occupied by students and certain empty properties. Exempt properties are: those which have been empty and unfurnished for 6 months; those left empty by someone entering hospital, a nursing home or residential care home; those left empty as a result of the death of the occupier and pending probate or letters of administration; those left empty for 6 months due to structural alterations. The owner is liable for the tax if the property is empty but not exempt, or if it is not the sole or main residence of the owner, such as a holiday home.

The persons liable

The tax is payable by the resident of a dwelling and that person may be the owner, leaseholder or licensee of the premises. Joint owners are jointly responsible for the tax. If there are no residents of properties not exempt, only the property element (50%) is payable. With one resident the tax is reduced by 25%.

Traders and landlords are relieved from the proportion of the charge applicable to the trade or the letting.

Reliefs

The following people living in a dwelling do not count as residents for the purpose of the tax: persons under 18; students; apprentices and VTS trainees; the severely impaired mentally. Residents who are disabled persons requiring extra space or rooms (such as downstairs bathrooms) are entitled to have the valuation of the premises placed in the next lower band, but there is no band lower than A. 80% of the tax is normally payable by persons receiving income support.

Payment by employer

Tax paid by an employer for an employee will be treated as a taxable benefit of the employee.

7.4 ERROR OR MISTAKE

It may happen that in completing his or her income tax return, the taxpayer makes a mistake which results in an excessive assessment. For example, an employed person may omit to claim the deduction of expenses wholly, exclusively and necessarily incurred in the performance of his duties; non-taxable capital receipts may have been included in business profits. Relief may be claimed for tax paid in respect of excessive assessments arising through an error or mistake, and claims may be made within six years from the end of the tax year during which the assessment was made. Relief is not given where the excessive assessment was made according to the practice then generally prevailing.

A taxpayer, finding that he has inadvertently made a mistake in a return or other statement resulting in the under-payment of tax, should immediately disclose the fullest details to his Inspector of Taxes, since failure to do so may well make it difficult to refute a more serious charge in the event of the Revenue authorities discovering the matter for themselves.

Where information supplied to the Inland Revenue has not been used by that body within a reasonable time, a proportion of the tax arrears is payable according to the following scale effective on 17 February 1993:

Taxpayer's gross income	*Proportion of tax remitted*
£15,500 or less	all
£15,501 to 18,000	3/4
£18,001 to 22,000	1/2
£22,001 to 26,000	1/4
£26,001 to 40,000	1/10
£40,001 and over	none

However, from the introduction of self-assessment in 1997 the submission of an incorrect, incomplete or late return will lead to the imposition of an automatic penalty. The penalty is £100 plus interest on tax paid late and on the penalty itself! Another penalty is levied every 6 months.

7.5 INCOME FROM ABROAD

The tax rules generally

The essential tax rules, which have many qualifications, but largely depend on residential status or domicile (see below), are as follows:

- UK residents are liable for UK tax on income and capital gains whether arising in the UK or elsewhere.
- Non-residents are liable for UK tax on income arising in the UK but

not on income arising outside the UK.
- Domicile affects inheritance tax and capital gains. For individuals domiciled in the UK inheritance tax is payable on assets wherever arising. Those not domiciled in the UK may incur liability to inheritance tax on UK assets; if they are resident in the UK they will not be liable to capital gains tax on a remittance basis.

The rules tend to be complex and, except in simple situations, merit expert advice.

European Economic Interest Groupings (EEIGS)

These bodies were set up under EEC regulations to carry out international business. For UK tax payers their profits are taxable and their losses allowable only in the hands of their members (FA 1990 S. 69 and Schedule 11). These bodies may be established in the European Union (EU) or the European Economic Area (EEA). The latter area includes Iceland and Norway.

Residence and domicile

Ordinary residence generally means living in the UK year after year on a permanent basis; but an individual who goes abroad permanently may still be regarded as ordinarily resident in the UK if visits to the UK are made 183 days or more in a tax year, or for an average of 91 days or more in each tax year calculated on a maximum of 4 years. Ordinary residence (but not 'residence') may be retained by going abroad for a holiday lasting more than a tax year, and certainly for visits abroad for less than a year.

An individual is strictly a 'resident' in the UK if he or she lives in the country for any period, but there are a number of exemptions for short visits – see Section 7.8. In particular the status of being resident applies (a) for a stay of 183 days or more in a tax year; (b) on coming to the UK permanently; (c) on coming to the UK for at least 3 years; and (d) a stay in the UK for employment for at least 2 years.

A taxpayer's domicile is his or her natural and permanent home. It affects liability to inheritance tax and capital gains tax. A domicile of origin applies to an individual at birth and is that of the father, or the mother of an illegitimate child or one whose father has died. This may be changed to a domicile of choice on attaining 16 years of age. Certain dependent people may be incapable of choosing a domicile and will assume a domicile of dependency.

Crown employees are liable to UK tax wherever they may reside.

Personal allowances

The general rule is that only individuals resident in the UK or Ireland are entitled to UK personal allowances. This rule is qualified by the fact that the following non-residents obtain full allowances:

- All citizens from European Economic Area (from 6 April 1996);
- Commonwealth citizens;
- Crown employees, including civil servants and members of the armed forces, and their widows or widowers;
- Employees of UK missionary societies:
- Residents in the Isle of Man or Channel Islands;
- Former residents in the UK who live abroad for health reasons and relatives who live with them;
- Where a double taxation agreement allows a claim to the allowance.

Temporary residence abroad

A person who leaves the UK for a stay abroad of less than a full tax year (6 April to the following 5 April) normally remains a UK resident for tax purposes. If, however, a person goes abroad for a complete tax year or longer to carry on a trade or profession, the UK residential status is lost from the date of leaving the UK although UK tax allowances continue to apply for the tax year of leaving. Where the person goes abroad for any other reason, UK residential status is retained until the habit of life indicates otherwise. The retention of a place of abode in the UK, a stay in the UK for 183 days or more in a tax year and visits to the UK for 91 days or more in any year, averaged over 5 years, are evidence that UK residential status has been retained.

Permanent residence abroad

Where an individual leaves the UK for permanent residence abroad the liability for UK tax is computed by reference to the period of residence in the UK. In other words, the tax year is split by the date of departure (and, if applicable, return). If such an individual returns to the UK before the end of the tax year following the tax year of departure the concession will not apply. The concession is extended to years of departure and return when an individual leaves the UK for full-time employment abroad for at least a complete tax year. Interim visits to the UK are limited to 183 days in a tax year or an average of 91 days over up to 4 years. Taxation of an accompanying spouse is also covered by this concession and it should be borne in mind that since 6 April 1990 married women are taxed independently from their husbands.

Non-residents – double taxation agreements

A person who is considered resident abroad is, in principle, liable to UK tax on income from the UK, but not on income from overseas sources. Such a person is also likely to be liable to the tax levied by the country of residence on his or her total income. Where, however, a double taxation agreement exists between the UK and the overseas country, double taxation is avoided by means of the following calculation:

(1) Calculate the tax which would be payable on the UK income alone, after deducting applicable UK allowances from that income.
(2) Calculate the UK tax which would be payable on the total income, UK as well as overseas income, after deducting UK allowances from that total income. Multiply the UK tax so calculated by the fraction:

$$\frac{\text{UK income}}{\text{Total income}}$$

(3) The UK tax payable is the greater of the amounts arrived at in (1) and (2) above and, unless the UK income is very large, will normally be the result of the second calculation.

Non-residents – tax-free interest

A further relief to non-residents is that they can arrange for interest on certain UK government stocks to be paid to them without deduction of UK tax; or if the tax has been deducted to claim repayment from the Inspector of Foreign Dividends. The stock in question includes: Exchequer Bonds, Funding Loan, Savings Bonds, Victory Bonds and 3½% War Stock.

Employment abroad with an overseas employer

Tax relief on foreign earnings was abolished by the 1998 budget, with effect from 17 March 1998 (Budget day). Prior to that, if a British resident was employed abroad by an overseas employer for 365 days or more, the whole of the overseas earnings is free of UK tax, but a return must be made to the UK authorities. In calculating the period abroad the taxpayer is allowed to count one-sixth of the period as continuous if he or she were on leave in the UK. In other words, if he or she spent more than one-sixth of the period on visits to the UK deduction from earnings would not be available. For a stay of 365 days or more abroad the period allowed in the UK is 62 days. The taxpayer is not assessed on certain expenses paid by the overseas employer, such as travel to and from the foreign country and hotel expenses. The remuneration from the overseas employer must be strictly applicable to the overseas employment.

Where, owing to the Gulf war, employees in Iraq or Kuwait had to return to the UK earlier than expected, they did not lose their exemption for foreign earnings.

Returning from overseas

The exemption from UK tax on foreign earnings basically applies to those who have retained their ordinary residence in the UK – that is, where the period abroad is short. Up to 5 April 1992 it was the practice of the Inland Revenue to give the exemption also to those who became ordinarily resident abroad as a result of a longer stay. But this practice ceased for those returning to the UK after 5 April 1992 so that terminal leave pay received in the UK after that date will be subject to UK tax. It may be possible to avoid this liability by arranging for the leave pay to be received while resident abroad or to have the leave period treated as residence abroad.

Overseas business or employment

Where a person is entitled to income from a trade, profession or vocation carried on abroad he or she will be assessable to UK tax on the whole of the income arising from that business. The assessment will be in the normal course on a preceding year basis (as applicable to an unincorporated business) and the taxpayer has the option of substituting the actual income of the period. It will be observed that an assessment on a business, i.e. Schedule D basis, would be preferable to one as an employee, on a Schedule E basis, because of the allowance of business expenses in the former case.

However, if the employee bears the cost of travel to and from his employment abroad, or the cost of board and lodgings abroad, that cost can be deducted from his salary under Schedule E. Similarly the cost of two journeys to and from abroad by a spouse or child under 18 to visit the taxpayer is deductible where the employee spends 60 days or more continuously abroad; so is the cost of two journeys by the taxpayer to the UK to see a spouse or child. In 1986/87 and onwards, if the employer pays the cost of travel, an unlimited number of journeys are tax free in the hands of the employee.

The Inland Revenue can in 1993/94 and onwards require the payer of an employee to collect tax under PAYE where the employee works for a person other than his or her employer. This applies where the employer is based either overseas or in the UK (T.A. 1988 S.203B).

In some cases the precise amount of taxable remuneration is not known at the time of payment to employees who work both in the UK and abroad. The taxable remuneration may have to be estimated when paid and subject to PAYE. This applies only to remuneration for UK duties for non-resident employees and also on remittances to the UK of payments for overseas duties in the case of employees who are not ordinarily resident in the UK.

Absence on business abroad

The foregoing provisions also until 1984/85 covered the case of an individual (including a partner) who was absent from the UK on business for at least 30 qualifying days. The relief applied to an individual who was resident in the UK and carried on a trade, profession or vocation chargeable to tax under Case I or Case II of Schedule D. The absence abroad must have been exclusively for the purpose of the business. The proportion of the income assessable is the proportion which the qualifying days abroad bear to 365 days. In the case of a partnership the income to be apportioned was the partner's share of the assessable partnership income after capital allowances but before loss relief.

Pensions from overseas sources

Where a UK resident receives a pension from overseas sources, and the British government has assumed responsibility for the payment, the whole amount of the pension is assessable in 1974/75 onwards, and not, as previously, merely the amount remitted to the UK. However, a deduction of 1/10th of the pension is allowed, or the whole of it for a pension payable for victims of National Socialist (Nazi) persecution in Germany or Austria.

7.6 INTEREST ON TAX

Interest on repayments

Interest, called a 'repayment supplement', is payable by the Inland Revenue in the case of a repayment of income tax or capital gains tax. If the repayment results from excess interim payments on account, interest will run from the actual dates the excess payments were received (i.e. usually around 31 January in the tax year and the following 31 July). To the extent the repayment results from an error in the balancing payment made on the 31 January following the tax year concerned, interest will run from this date as well.

Interest is also due on a repayment to a company of corporation tax, tax credits or investment income, or tax suffered by deduction. In this case the repayment is made after the end of 12 months from the latest date when the corporation tax was payable on the company's profits. The individual company must be resident in the UK. The interest is not taxable.

Interest on tax overdue

Subject to some special exceptions, interest is chargeable on tax unpaid. Historically interest below £30 was not charged but the use of computers now allows the increased ability to charge for *all* late payments of tax. The interest is not an allowable expense for tax purposes.

7.7 DISCRETIONARY AND ACCUMULATION TRUSTS

Income of discretionary and accumulation trusts, and capitals gains, is chargeable at 34% since 1996/97. When a beneficiary receives a payment of income from the trust he or she obtains a tax credit of the overall rate applying at the time of payment. From 6 April 1995 bank interest payable to these trusts from UK banks was subject to deduction of tax at the basic rate of 25% – from 6 April 1996 at the lower rate of 20%. But the trustee must account for the extra 14% (34% - 20%).

From 6 April 1995 the rules applicable to the taxation of trust income have been simplified and will be essentially as follows:

- If the settlor or the settlor's spouse has retained an interest in the trust, the income will be treated as that of the settlor for tax purposes.
- The income will also be treated as that of the settlor where the trust or settlement is in favour of the settlor's minor unmarried child.
- Where the settlor or the settlor's spouse receives a loan from the trustees, or makes a loan to them, the settlor will be liable to income tax on the annual value of the loan, by reference to a statutory rate of interest.

7.8 VISITORS TO THE UK

Individuals covered

This section gives a general guide to the position of foreign-domiciled nationals who stay in the UK for substantial periods and receive income here. It also applies to British nationals when they return to the UK after long periods abroad, having meanwhile lost their UK residential status. The subject tends to be specialised and in a complicated situation expert advice is desirable.

Residence

The crucial question is whether the visitor is considered to have become resident in the UK. The general rules covering residence in the UK are as follows:

- An individual is not to be considered resident in the UK if here for a temporary purpose only, but will be regarded as resident if he or she spends more than 183 days here in any tax year to 5 April.
- Residence in the UK will be assumed if the individual visits the UK year after year for three years, spending three months here each year.

- Before 6 April 1993 residence in the UK was assumed where a visitor has a place of abode here, unless he or she works full time outside the UK, and in the later case duties performed in the UK are only incidental to the overseas employment. On and after 6 April 1993 the existence of available accommodation is ignored in determining residential status.
- Where a visitor acquires a lease of three years or more for accommodation in the UK he or she will become ordinarily resident from the following dates:
  (i) From the date of arrival if the lease is acquired in the tax year of arrival;
  (ii) From the beginning of the tax year of acquiring the lease if acquired after the tax year of arrival.

Where there is no intention of remaining in the UK for three years, and no three-year lease of accommodation is acquired, the visitor does not become ordinarily resident until the beginning of the tax year after the third anniversary of arrival.

UK tax liability

- Non-residents. No UK tax is payable on income, e.g. pay, arising overseas. Income arising in the UK is, however, liable for UK tax at the basic rate and no personal allowances can be obtained.
- Residents. Individuals becoming resident here are liable for UK tax and are entitled to full personal allowances for the tax year in which they arrive.

Liability to UK tax is computed by reference to the period of residence in the following situations:

- Where an individual takes up permanent residence in the UK or intends to stay in the UK for at least three years.
- Where an individual takes up employment in the UK expected to last for at least two years.
- An individual who becomes resident in the UK is liable to capital gains tax on gains accruing after arrival in the UK and before departure.

7.9 INSURANCE PREMIUM TAX

This tax was imposed on 1 October 1994. Exemptions include certain long-term insurances, such as life insurance, export credit insurance and insurance of specific means of transport such as ships, aircraft and railway rolling stock. It increased in most cases from 4% to 5% on 1 July 1999. However a higher rate of 17.5% does apply to mechanical breakdown insurance (e.g. TV repair cover), travel insurance and car hire insurance.This is due to the abuse by some retailers of moving monies into insurance products from the main supply because of the lower duty.

7.10 AIR PASSENGER DUTY

From 1 November 1997, passengers travelling by air from UK airports are charged a duty of £10 (previously £5) per passenger for destinations in the European Union (EU) or European Economic Area (EEA), and £20 (previously £10) for destinations elsewhere. The £10 (previously £5) rate applies to destinations in Iceland and Norway, to return journeys in the UK and to Basle and Geneva.

From April 2001, the duty on economy flights within the EEA will be reduced to £5. In addition, no duty will be levied on flights from airports in the Scottish Highlands and Islands.

But, from April 2000, the duty exemptions for return flights within the UK will be removed. The rates of duty for those travelling first or club class within the EEA will remain at £10 but will rise to £40 for flights to destinations outside the EEA.

CHAPTER 8

VALUE ADDED TAX

8.1 THE GENERAL NATURE OF THE TAX

VAT came into effect for transactions made on and after 1 April 1973 and replaced purchase tax and the selective employment tax. The legislation is contained in the Value Added Tax Act 1994, as amended by the subsequent Finance Acts, and detailed provisions set out in numerous statutory orders issued from time to time.

The rate for all taxable goods and services not zero-rated became 17½% from 1 April 1991.

VAT is a common method of indirect taxation in the European Union and, subject to variations of treatment amongst the member States, is made obligatory by a Directive of the Council of the EU. In the UK it takes the form of a charge on the invoiced value of applicable goods and services made by traders who are not exempt. The amount so charged to customers may be set against the VAT suffered by the trader on his or her purchases; in some cases this calculation may lead to a repayment of tax to the trader. The tax suffered by a business on its purchases is called 'input tax' and that which it charges its customers is called the 'output tax'.

The system operates right through the chain of importation or production of goods, through the distribution via wholesalers, until the final sale from the retailer to the consumer. It is thus the ultimate consumer who bears the tax on the sale price of purchases. As will be seen from the example below, the tax eventually takes the form of a tax on value added to basic raw materials or services.

Some goods and services are 'exempt' from the tax, and this means that the trader will not be able to charge the tax on sales to customers nor be able to obtain a credit for 'input tax' on relevant purchases. Exemption from all goods sold also applies to traders with a turnover of no more than £52 000 from 1 April 2000 (£51 000 previously) but exemption may not be an advantage since, although they cannot charge their customers with the tax, they are unable to claim credit for input tax suffered.

Many categories of goods and services are 'zero-rated'. This also means that the trader dealing in such goods cannot charge customers with the tax but can claim credit for relevant input tax.

8.2 THE SYSTEM ILLUSTRATED

Assuming that the goods are taxable and not zero-rated, and that the traders concerned are not exempt but are 'registered' with the Customs and Excise, the system, in its simplest form, may be illustrated as follows:

	£	£
1. A manufacturer buys raw materials at a basic price of	1000	
on which his supplier charges VAT at 17½%, i.e.	175	
giving a cost to the manufacturer of	1 175	
2. The manufacturer sells to a wholesaler goods produced from the raw materials at a basic price of	2 000	
to which he adds VAT of	350	
the wholesaler paying	2 350	
3. The manufacturer pays to the Customs and Excise VAT on his invoice	350	
Less: VAT on his purchase	175	
a net payment of		175
4. The wholesaler sells the goods to a retailer at	2 800	
plus VAT	490	
the retailer paying	3 290	
5. The wholesaler pays to the Customs and Excise: VAT on his invoice	490	
Less: VAT on his purchase	350	
a net payment of		140
6. The retailer sells to the consumer at	4 200	
plus VAT	735	
the consumer paying	4 935	
7. The retailer pays to the Customs and Excise: VAT on his sale	735	
Less: VAT on his purchase	490	
a net payment of		245
The total tax to Customs is		560
This represents 17½% on the value added to the raw material, i.e. 17½% (£4 200–£1 000)		560

8.3 TAXABLE SUPPLIES

VAT is payable only where there is a taxable supply, i.e. the goods or services are those covered by the tax and are not exempt or zero-rated. VAT is payable on imports of taxable goods as though it were a customs duty, and it may be payable by a UK agent who is working on commission for an overseas principal.

Goods produced by a business or acquired by a business and used for the purposes of that business, e.g. stationery printed in the business, are taxable at market value. This is the process known for VAT purposes as 'self supply'. Where, however, goods are produced by a business or acquired by a business and applied by the owner for personal use, the cost of those goods is taxable. Cost is not defined for this purpose but, in the case of manufactured articles, it is thought to mean direct cost, e.g. materials and labour, plus manufacturing overheads.

Samples and promotional gifts are taxable at the cost to the supplier but if that cost is no more than £15 they will be tax free. VAT can be recovered on the cost of gifts over the limit if they are accompanied by a certificate indicating that output tax will be accounted for. Industrial samples for testing and market research are also tax free, whatever their cost or value, provided they are not of the kind obtainable in the market place.

Goods supplied on hire purchase are taxable on their cash price, i.e. excluding interest or hire purchase charges, which are not subject to VAT.

Goods and services will be taxed net of cash discount, provided the rate is shown on the invoice and whether or not the discount is taken by the customer.

For retailers using the standard basis, VAT is paid on cash received, so that bad debts are automatically relieved of the tax. With the alternative basis, VAT is paid on credit sales invoiced plus cash sales.

8.4 THE TAX POINT

This is the point when liability to the tax arises, although the actual payment or repayment of tax may not be due until some months later. Basically the tax point is when the goods are despatched or made available to the customer, but the tax point may be extended to the date when the invoice is issued within 14 days of the despatch of the goods. The Commissioners are authorised to agree special arrangements as to the tax point with particular traders.

In the case of goods on sale or return, the tax point is when the goods have finally been accepted by the customer, but this date must not be more than 12 months after despatch to the customer.

In the case of goods on hire (not hire purchase or credit sale) the tax point is when each successive payment becomes due, and such point may be expressed in the agreement, or when an invoice is issued, if earlier.

For goods on hire purchase the tax point is when the goods are supplied.

8.5 ADMINISTRATION

Registration

A trader is obliged to register for VAT with the Customs and Excise where turnover exceeds £52 000 from 1 April 2000 (previously £51 000 from 1 April 1999). On registration the trader must show on the invoices issued the tax added to the relevant charges, except in the case of retailers making cash sales; and must make normally quarterly returns, paying or reclaiming the difference between input and output tax. It could, however, be advantageous to register, even though turnover is expected to be below the limit, where input tax was likely to be less than output tax and the difference could be reclaimed. Registration can be cancelled where turnover is below the limit of £50 000 from 1 April 2000 (previously £49 000 from 1 April 1999).

However, these limits may be decreased in the future. There is currently a review of the limits; the registration limits in other EU countries are far lower than in the UK.

Records and tax invoices

All traders who are not exempt are obliged to keep records of their purchases and sales including records of the VAT applicable on those transactions. They are also obliged to keep what is called a 'tax account' in which their total liabilities or claims in respect of VAT are recorded. No particular form of record or account is specified. The authorities have the right to inspect records (including computer operations) and tax invoices and may obtain the power to enter premises for this purpose. Special regulations apply to the records of retailers.

All non-exempt traders, except retailers making cash sales, must issue what are called 'tax invoices' on making sales. A tax invoice is simply an ordinary invoice which contains certain specified information, i.e. the usual invoice details plus: the number of the invoice, the registered number of the supplier, the type of supply (e.g. whether zero-rated, etc.) and the tax charged. Exempt and zero-rated supplies must be separated even though they are included in one invoice with taxable goods. Invoices need not be issued for zero-rated supplies, second-hand goods relieved of tax, gifts, and goods for which input tax is not deducted.

Returns and payments

Returns showing the input and output tax for the period must normally be submitted to the Customs and Excise at specified three-monthly intervals, and these claims will show the amount of tax to be paid or repaid. Where the business is likely to obtain a repayment, application may be made for the returns and the settlement to be made monthly, thus helping to improve the cash flow of the business. From 1991/92 businesses with a turnover below £300 000 (previously £250 000) can opt for annual accountancy subject to nine estimated payments in advance, with a tenth adjusting payment.

If returns are not made or they are inaccurate, the authorities may make an estimated assessment on the trader. Such an assessment must be made within six years after the end of the accounting period concerned but cannot be made after three years from the death of the trader. The trader may appeal against an assessment to the Commissioners and thence to a quasi judicial body, independent of the Commissioners, known as a VAT tribunal.

Penalties

Penalties, fines and interest may be payable for failure to comply with the VAT legislation. In the case of failure to pay the amount due the authorities have the ultimate power of obtaining a distress warrant with a view to the sale of the taxpayer's goods, furniture and other chattels. From 11 March 1992 a penalty will not normally be imposed unless the net VAT underdeclared or overpaid exceeds £2 000 in an accounting period.

Serious misdeclarations are those where on one return 30% of the tax managed (input and output) is underdeclared; or more than £1 million. From 11 March 1992 the penalty in such cases was reduced from 20% to 15% and a period of grace is normally given if the misdeclaration is rectified in the next return. A default surcharge applies to late returns and late payments on three occasions, the maximum penalty being 15%.

Cash accounting

Registered persons must inform the Customs and Excise for VAT to be based on the amounts paid and received during a quarterly or monthly accounting period. This system can simplify the accounting requirements for many of the smaller businesses and, where substantial credit is given to customers, improve the cash flow. Bad debts are automatically accounted for by failure to receive the amount due. It could be a disadvantage in terms of cash flow when tax receivable on purchases is higher than tax payable on sales and where long terms of credit are taken on supplies.

Cash accounting is available where turnover is not expected to exceed £350 000 in the year from 1 April 1993 (previously £300 000), and can continue until turnover reaches £437 500. The VAT outstanding must not exceed £5 000. It operates from the beginning of the normal tax period for the business and must be continued for at least two years. Transactions excluded from a cash accounting system are: imports, exports, hire purchase, conditional and credit sales.

Tax invoices must continue to be kept and, for cash (not cheque) payments, they need to be receipted. Receipts and payments by credit card are entered at the date of the invoice, but giro transactions, standing orders and direct debits at the date of entry in the bank account. Part payments or receipts should be related to specific invoices.

8.6 EXEMPT TRADERS

These are (a) small traders with a turnover of no more than £52 000 from 1 April 2000 (previously £51 000 from 1 April 1999), and (b) traders who deal only with exempt supplies. The first category need not register, do not have to charge VAT on their sales, and are not liable to account for VAT, but they cannot recover from the Customs and Excise the VAT charged on their purchases. They can register voluntarily and if they do so they are no longer exempt. The second category of trader cannot obtain refunds of input tax, but where there are both taxable and exempt supplies a proportion of the input tax is refundable.

8.7 EXEMPT GOODS AND SERVICES

A large number of kinds of goods and services are exempt from VAT – that is to say, VAT cannot be charged when such goods are sold, even by a registered trader. These categories are summarised below.

Group 1 The grant of any interest in or right over land but not the letting of accommodation, parking or camping facilities or fishing or taking game. Bedroom accommodation in hotels is taxable but not other accommodation in hotels, or elsewhere. From 1 August 1989 an election (subject to many qualifications) can be made to waive this exemption, and thus recover input tax.

Group 2 Insurance, covering also services provided by brokers and agents; but most marine, aviation and transport insurance is zero-rated. Note that insurance premium tax at 3% was imposed from 1 October 1994.

Group 3 Postal services, but not cable services.

Group 4 Betting, gaming and lotteries, but admission charges, club subscriptions and takings from gaming machines are taxable.

Group 5 Finance, i.e. dealing in money or credit, banking and the sale of securities, but stockbrokers' commissions and unit trust management fees are taxable. The charge made by credit card companies on retailers is exempt. where banks buy in credit card processing, the charge for this service will no longer be exempt from 9 March 1999 (Budget Day).

Group 6 Education, including the supply of incidental services and covering the facilities provided by youth clubs and similar organisations.

Group 7 Health, covering goods and services provided by medical practitioners, dentists, opticians (the eye test is exempt, as is carrying out the resulting prescription, but the provision of spectacles is not), nurses, pharmaceutical chemists, hearing aid dispensers, hospitals, etc. Protective boots and helmets purchased by businesses are chargeable from 1 April 1989.

Group 8 Burial and cremation services.

Group 9 Trade unions and professional bodies.

Group 10 Sports competitions and physical education.

Group 11 Works of art, etc. Disposals exempt from capital gains tax. (See also under Section 8.9.)

Group 12 Fundraising by charities.

Group 13 Cultural services, etc.

From 1 April 1992 the salary foregone is exempt from VAT when employees opt to use a company car instead of salary. From 1 April 1993 Government-funded training courses are exempt.

8.8 ZERO-RATED SUPPLIES

Zero-rating means that, although the goods are theoretically taxable, the rate of tax is nil. Because zero-rated goods are taxable, suppliers of these goods can recover tax they have suffered on relevant purchases; they do not, however, charge tax on their sales of zero-rated goods. All goods exported by a registered trader are zero-rated, but not in 1985/86 and onwards goods exported or imported for processing and re-exported. Other zero-rated supplies are set out in Schedule 8 VAT Act 1994, subsequent statutory orders, and the Finance Act 1989, and these groups are summarised below.

Group 1 Food for human consumption, including many packaged goods, animal feeding stuffs, but not soft drinks (it has now been held that freshly-pressed citrus fruits are zero-rated), alcoholic drinks, confectionery, ice-cream, petfoods, seeds, and animals yielding food for human consumption. There are many exemptions to the above.

Group 2 Water, other than distilled water, and sewerage services except when supplied to businesses from 1 July 1990.

Group 3 Publications such as books, newspapers, periodicals, music, maps, etc., but not stationery.

Group 4 Talking books, radio sets, boats, maintenance of 'talking books', recorders and magnetic tape and radio sets for use by the blind and handicapped. From 1 April 1986 much other equipment for handicapped persons or charities was zero-rated, including lifts, alarms and welfare vehicles; from 1 April 1989 medical sterilising equipment for charities; and from 1 April 1992 toilet facilities in charitable buildings.

Group 5 Construction of dwellings, residential accommodation and charitable purposes and the grant of a major interest in the property, including sale of the freehold or grant of lease for over 21 years, but only when the trader is the person constructing the building. Residential accommodation includes homes for children, the aged and infirm, students, the armed forces, monasteries and nunneries. In accordance with EU law the construction of new industrial and commercial buildings will be subject to VAT for contracts made after 1 April 1989. The letting for one or two weeks in a year of time-share holiday homes by a long lease is not zero-rated (Cottage Holiday Assoc. Ltd. v Customs and Excise, 1982). Note that land is exempt and that the maintenance of buildings is chargeable at the VAT rate. From 1 June 1984 VAT applies to structural alterations, sheds and greenhouses in private gardens, and fixtures in new buildings, but not to substantial conversion, alteration and enlargement of ancient monuments and listed buildings. From 1 April 1986 zero-rating applied to building alterations for the benefit of a resident handicapped person.

Landlords can opt to charge VAT on non-residential rents from 1 August 1989. In this case tenants pay tax on half the rents in the first year, or for five years where they are charities.

Group 6 Protected buildings.

Group 7 Services to overseas traders or for overseas purposes.

Group 8 Transport, covering the supply, services and maintenance of ships above 15 tons and not used for recreational purposes; and aircraft above 18,000 pounds and not used for recreation; and the transport of passengers in vehicles carrying 12 or more passengers (i.e. excluding taxis). Airline meals are not taxable.

Group 9 Caravans above the limits for use as trailers (i.e. 22.9 feet in length or 7.5 feet in width) and houseboats.

Group 10 Gold bullion and gold coins, when supplied by a Central Bank to another Central Bank or to and from a Central Bank to a member of the London Gold Market. The Finance Act 1993 s45 provides that on and after 1 April 1993 where any person makes a supply of gold for business purposes that supply is a taxable supply, but not a zero-rated supply. Where the supplier is a taxable person and the supplies are made in connection with the business of the customer, the latter (i.e. the purchaser) must account for and pay tax on the supply on the supplier's behalf. The supplies may consist of gold, gold coins and goods containing gold, taxable at the open market value of the gold contained in the goods.

Group 11 Bank notes.

Group 12 Drugs, medicines and appliances supplied on prescription, whether under the National Health Service or otherwise including from 10 March 1981 ambulances and wheelchairs supplied to hospitals and car adaptations for the disabled; also in 1984/85 and onwards cars leased to disabled persons under mobility schemes; in 1985/86 medical and scientific equipment, including computers, donated to hospitals; in 1986/87 bathroom equipment for the handicapped in charitable residential homes, and equipment for charitable first aid and rescue services.

Group 13 Imports and exports subject to qualifications.

Group 14 Tax-free shops

Group 15 Charities. Much equipment used or supplied by charities is zero-rated (see also under Group 4) and zero-rating is applied to medicinal products supplied to a charity for medical research, both for humans and animals – see Value Added Tax (Handicapped Persons and Charities Order) 1986. Also, from 1 April 1991 television, radio and cinema advertising, donated goods, and equipment for veterinary research.

Group 16 Clothing for young children, industrial safety clothing and motor cycle crash helmets.

Also zero-rated from 1 April 1993 are protective boots and helmets and parts and equipment for certain ships and aircraft not used for recreation.

8.9 THE LOWER 5% RATE

VAT on domestic fuel was reduced to 5% in 1997. The budget in March 2000 introduced two more proposals for the 5% band.

(a) A cut in the rate of VAT applicable to domestic energy saving materials has been announced. The 5% rate applies to the supply *and* installation of energy saving materials such as insulation, draught stripping, hot water and central heating system controls, as well as solar panels, to all homes. This is introduced from 1 April 2000 but does not apply to the DIY market.

(b) The VAT rate applicable to women's sanitary products is to be reduced from 17.5% to 5% from 1 January 2001.

8.10 MISCELLANEOUS

- **Local authorities** (and similar bodies) are entitled to refunds of VAT suffered on purchases in relation to non-business activities.
- **Business entertainment.** Tax suffered on business entertaining cannot be deducted from output tax. Tax on allowable subsistence for business purposes is, however, deductible from output tax.
- **Hotel accommodation, catering and tourism.** Up to four weeks accommodation, including board and service, is taxable at the current VAT rate. After four weeks the charge for the rent of the room or rooms is not taxable. The charge for the use of services will be assumed to be not less than 20% of the accommodation charge excluding meals. The charge for meals will also bear the current rate. Gross profits by tour operators on tours in the European Union are taxable.
- **Trophies.** VAT was not separately payable on the cost of trophies awarded at a presentation dinner when VAT was paid on receipts from ticket sales (Commissioners of Customs and Excise v. Professional Footballers' Association Ltd., TLR 1993. House of Lords).
- **Second-hand Goods.** From 1 January 1995 the margin scheme of VAT applies to all second-hand goods, works of art, antiques and collectors' items but not to precious metals and gem stones.
- **Imports.** From 1 January 1995 imports of certain works of art, antiques and collectors' items are charged VAT at 2.5%.

8.11 MOTOR CARS

VAT

VAT is charged by the seller on the price charged to the buyer and is reclaimable by a dealer whose business it is to sell cars, and by companies buying their own cars wholly for business use (from 1 August 1995).

Reclaiming VAT

An individual or company buying a car for use in the business, or for private use, cannot reclaim the tax which it has paid to the dealer or on importing the car, but from 1 August 1992 the VAT can be reclaimed by taxi firms, self-drive hire firms and driving schools, subject to adjustment for personal use. From 1 January 1994 VAT can be recovered by businesses leasing cars to these activities.

Vehicles chargeable to VAT

These are essentially private type cars for use on public roads and constructed or adapted for carrying passengers. Vehicles not chargeable are those accommodating only one, or more than twelve, passengers; of above 3 tonnes unladen weight; caravans, ambulances, prison vans, approved taxi cabs; and special vehicles not for carrying passengers, such as ice-cream vans, mobile shops and offices, hearses and bullion vans. VAT is payable when an exempt vehicle is converted to carry passengers. Cars used by manufacturers for research and development are relieved from VAT from 1 April 1989. From 29 July 1989 exemption was extended to cars leased to handicapped persons, and to members of visiting forces and to individuals with diplomatic privileges.

Leasing and hire purchase

VAT must be paid on the sale price when a car is acquired by hire purchase and can be reclaimed by a dealer. If a car is leased VAT must be charged on the rentals and can be reclaimed by the lessor if in business, but only 50% where any use of the car is made for private motoring (Budget 1994). Vehicles purchased for leasing to the disabled are relieved from car tax from 1 April 1989. (See also under 'Reclaiming VAT' above.) No refunds of VAT can be claimed where businesses buy company cars on long leases from EU suppliers who do not conduct business in the UK.

Repairs and maintenance

VAT is chargeable on the cost and can be reclaimed in full by a business even if there is some private use.

Sale of used cars

Basically VAT must be charged on the sale price of used cars, whether sold by a dealer or by a business using the car for the business. However, the special scheme applicable to such sales enables the VAT to be charged only on the excess of the selling price over the purchase price of the car. No tax invoice is issued and the input tax cannot be reclaimed.

Fuel benefit

This is the scale charge for income tax on fuel provided free or below cost to employees for their private mileage. The benefit is subject to VAT from 6 April 1987, and is calculated on the tax-inclusive charge.

Car fuel scale rates

Where VAT is reclaimed on fuel used for private purposes VAT according to scale is added to the output tax. It may not be beneficial to reclaim VAT on fuel if the amount so claimed is less than the scale charge.

8.12 RETAILERS

Retailers are not obliged to prepare tax invoices unless they are demanded by customers, and hence a number of special schemes for accounting for VAT are available for retailers and are set out in Notice 727 issued by the Customs and Excise. The availability of these schemes is to be drastically restricted following the Budget in 1996.

8.13 BAD DEBTS

Normally, where a supplier has suffered a bad debt incurred by an insolvent customer, the supplier can reclaim VAT he has already paid on the supplies concerned. The sale must have been at open-market value and the property in the goods must have passed. The supplier must prove in the bankruptcy, or liquidation in the case of a limited company, for the debt less the VAT. By the exercise of an option for cash accounting, where turnover is below £350 000, bad debts will be automatically relieved from VAT. From 1 April 1993 VAT can be reclaimed on bad debts which are more than six months old based on date of supply (previously one year old) and have been written off in the trader's accounts; from 6 October 1997 relief for bad debts is available for barter transactions; the relief can be back-dated to when the debt arose. A three-year limit is to be put on the age of the bad debt. The Customs and Excise will also attempt to recollect the VAT from the debtor business.

8.14 DIRECTORS' ACCOMMODATION

From 1990/91 VAT is no longer recoverable on costs, such as repairs, incurred on accommodation provided by companies for directors or their families.

8.15 TREATMENT FOR INCOME AND CORPORATION TAX

Persons exempt from VAT

Allowable business expenses can include VAT charged on purchases, etc.

Other persons

Income and expenditure is to be brought into the tax computation exclusive of VAT.

8.16 SINGLE EUROPEAN MARKET

From 1 January 1993 border controls between members of the European Union (EU) are largely abolished.

Before 1 January 1993 controls of imports and exports were carried out by Customs and Exercise at the frontiers. As a result the exporter had to claim customs clearance for zero-rating on the shipment of goods and for imports before the goods were released by customs.

From 1 January 1993 VAT is charged, if applicable, not on the importation of goods but on the acquisition from other EU states. The tax point of 'acquisition' is the 15th of the month following acquisition, or the date of the invoice. Where goods pass from an EU state to a non-EU state controls at the border will remain. To obtain zero-rating of exports the supplier must show on his invoice not only his UK VAT registration number but also that of his customer in the importing state, and submit to the Customs a quarterly list of such exports.

Where customers are not VAT-registered sales up to various limits (depending on the EU state concerned) are chargeable to VAT. Above these limits VAT is payable in the importing state and this may involve appointing a VAT representative in that state.

The members of the EU are: the UK, Austria, Finland, Sweden, Germany, France, Italy, Spain, Belgium, Portugal, Denmark, Greece, Ireland, Luxemburg and the Netherlands.

New legislation is contained in the Finance Act (No. 2) 1992 and various statutory instruments.

CHAPTER 9

INHERITANCE TAX

9.1 GENERAL NATURE OF THE TAX

This is the tax on the value of estates passing on the death of an individual and on gifts made seven years before death. The tax applies when the total value of the estate and the chargeable gifts exceeds £234 000 in 2000/01 (£231 000 in 1999/00) for deaths and the rate is 40%. Subject to the many exemptions indicated below, the amount chargeable to the tax includes the value of property both in and outside the UK where the deceased was domiciled in the UK; but only property in the UK is valued for those domiciled elsewhere, although in such cases double taxation relief may apply.

The Finance Act 1986 gave the new title of 'inheritance tax' to what was previously called 'capital transfer tax'. The latter tax was not repealed but was substantially amended, particularly by the elimination of tax on most lifetime gifts. The amended provisions apply to deaths after 17 March 1986 and gifts or transfers made after that date.

The following sections cover only the essentials of inheritance tax, which represents a very complex body of legislation. For more detailed information it will be necessary to obtain expert professional advice.

9.2 EXEMPTIONS

- Property passing on death and seven years before death up to a value of £234 000 in 2000/01 (£231 000 in 1999/00).
- Transfers or gifts between husband and wife made on death or at any time previously, subject to a limit of £55 000 if the recipient is domiciled abroad.
- Gifts which represent normal expenditure out of income.
- Lifetime gifts in consideration of (i.e. before) marriage: those by the parents of the married couple up to £5 000; by a remoter ancestor up to £2 500; and by others up to £1 000.
- Gifts to charities, for national purposes and the national benefit; also gifts to political parties.
- Cash options to widows and dependants under approved annuity schemes and certain overseas pensions.
- Tax-free government securities in the beneficial ownership of persons not domiciled or ordinarily resident in the UK; and all property outside the UK owned by such persons.
- Gifts for the maintenance or education of a spouse, child or dependant.
- Majority holdings of shares given to employees on trust.

- Legacies disclaimed within two years of death.
- Lifetime transfers up to £3 000 a year, this limit excluding the small gifts exemption of £250 a year.
- Bona fide transfers of property in the course of trade for adequate consideration and allowable for income tax.
- Where death was attributable to injury or disease arising from active service with the armed forces.

9.3 THE VALUE TRANSFERRED

Where a specific sum of money is given, either on death or during lifetime, the value transferred is the amount of money in question. In the case of transfers of other assets, such as investments, jewellery, furniture, land and buildings, the asset will need to be valued at market value at the date of transfer. More strictly the value to be taken into account is the loss in value to the donor.

Transfers of shares in unquoted companies made within seven years before death (except to a wife) should be made at a freely negotiated price, so that no chargeable benefit arises.

The gross value of the estate at death may include interests in applicable trusts, such as discretionary trusts and sums due to the estate, such as under life policies and death benefit under pensions schemes. From the gross value of the estate deductions are made for debts, including income tax due at death, and funeral expenses, but not executorship expenses.

Other lifetime transfers which are not potentially exempt transfers (see below) are chargeable at half the full rate. Where death occurs within 7 years the balance of the full rate becomes payable, subject to tapering relief (see below).

9.4 GIFTS WITHIN SEVEN YEARS OF DEATH

Up to 17 March 1986 chargeable gifts and transfers made within 10 years of death were chargeable to tax at the lifetime rate of capital transfer tax. Gifts made after 17 March 1986 within seven years of death will be chargeable to the appropriate rate of inheritance tax, subject to 'tapering relief' – see below.

9.5 TAPERING RELIEF

The tax payable on chargeable gifts or transfers made within three to seven years of death is reduced or 'tapered' according to the following scale:

Period before death	*Proportion of tax rate payable*
6 to 7 years	20%
5 to 6 years	40%
4 to 5 years	60%
3 to 4 years	80%
up to 3 years	full rate

9.6 POTENTIALLY EXEMPT TRANSFERS (PET)

These are transfers which will only become chargeable if death occurs within seven years after they are made. They include gifts to individuals and accumulation and maintenance trusts set up for members of the deceased's family or for the disabled. They do not include discretionary settlements.

Where a PET becomes a chargeable transfer because of death the tax payable on it is determined by any gifts made in the 7 years prior to that gift. This means that any gift made in the 14 years before death will either incur a direct liability (within 7 years of death) or increase the liability on a gift inside the 7-year period (if such a gift is made within 7 years of the first gift).

For example, let us suppose that Anne gives her son £150 000 in October 1985. No tax is payable because it is a PET. She gives £150 000 to her daughter in September 1988. No tax is payable on this either as it is a PET. Her daughter had got married three months earlier. Anne gives £35,000 each to her two grandchildren in November 1993. No tax is payable at this time because the gifts are PETs. She dies in August 1996, when her estate is £250,000.

The gift to her son is completely exempt because it was made more than 7 years before her death. The gift to her daughter is also exempt because it was made more than 7 years before her death. The gifts to the grandchildren are chargeable because they were made in the 7 years before her death. The tax payable will be determined by adding these gifts to the gift to the daughter which was made in the previous 7 years (the gift to her son was made more than 7 years before the gift to the grandchildren). To determine the IHT payable on the estate at the date of death it will be necessary to add its value to that of the gifts to the grandchildren but not the two earlier gifts which are outside the chargeable period.

How much tax will Anne pay?

(i) IHT payable by Anne's grandchildren on their gifts

Amount of gifts (Nov 93)	£70 000
Less yearly gift allowance 92/3 and 93/4	(£6 000)
Chargeable	£64 000

Added to:		
Value of gift to daughter (Sep 88)	£150 000	
Less yearly gift allowance 88/89 and 87/88 (unused and brought forward)	(£6 000)	
Chargeable		£144 000
Total chargeable		£208 000
Less £200 000 limit (for 1996/97)		(£200 000)
Net chargeable		£8 000
Net tax payable by grandchildren at 40%		£3 200

Each grandchild will now have to find £1 600 within 6 months of Anne's death (i.e. by 28 February 1997). The gifts were made within three years of Anne's death, so there is no tapering relief. If they had been given the money a year earlier, in November 1992, tapering relief would have operated, and the total tax payable would have been £2 560 (£3 200 x 80%).

(ii) IHT payable on Anne's estate

Estate at death		£250 000
Added to: value of gifts to grandchildren (Nov 93)	£70 000	
Less yearly gift allowance 92/93 and 93/94	(£6 000)	
		£66 000
Chargeable		£314 000
Less £200 000 limit (for 1996/97)		(£200 000)
Net chargeable		£114 000
Net tax payable by executors of estate at 40%		£45 600

So Anne doesn't leave £250,000; her beneficiaries will receive only £204 400.

By using the annual reliefs every year, and the £5 000 exemption available when her daughter got married (the gift was after the marriage and not in 'anticipation') she could have reduced the tax payable on the November 1993 gift and on her death. Note that an insurance policy could also have been taken out at the time of the gifts to cover the potential tax liability both to Anne's grandchildren and to her estate.

9.7 GIFTS WITH RESERVATIONS

These are gifts made after 17 March 1986 with a reservation for the donor to obtain a benefit. Examples of reservations would be the retention of a right to obtain income or enjoy the gifted property, to continue to live in a gifted house, inheritance trusts and insurance policies for the mitigation of the tax.

A gift with reservations to an individual will be taxed on the death of the donor, but one made to a trust or company will be taxed when it is made. Tax will be charged on the gift when the reservation is released, or the enjoyment of the property ceases, e.g. on the death of the donor, subject to credit for any tax already paid. Exceptions include the case where reasonable provision is made for a relative who becomes unable to maintain himself or herself after the gift was made.

9.8 OTHER RELIEFS

The more important other reliefs are as follows:

Businesses

From 10 March 1992 100% relief (previously 50%) applies to interests in unincorporated businesses (e.g. those of a sole owner or partnership); and to (from 28 November 1995 to all holdings held for more than 2 years) holdings above 25% in unquoted companies, excluding those on the Unlisted Securities Market (USM) or its successor.

50% relief applies to controlling interests in fully quoted companies; up to 27 November 1995 holdings under 25% in unquoted companies; and assets owned by partners or controlling shareholders and used in their partnerships or companies.

The relief applies to market makers on the Stock Exchange and the London International Futures and Options Exchange from 23 March 1992. Otherwise dealers in investments are excluded from the relief and so are dealers in land.

Agricultural land

100% relief from inheritance tax is available, subject to conditions, for agricultural land passing after 10 March 1992 (previously 50%). The main conditions are:

- That the property was occupied by the deceased (or transferor) for the purpose of agriculture throughout the period of two years before death or transfer;
- That the property was owned by the deceased (or transferor) for seven years before death (or transfer) and occupied for that purpose

by the deceased (or transferor) or by another person;

- The relief applies to leases of agricultural land at full market value; from 28 November 1995 relief is available for farmland subject to agricultural tenancies acquired as a result of the death of the previous tenant. The death must have occurred on or after 1 September 1995.
- In all other cases the relief is at 50%.
- The 1996 Budget introduced relief for land dedicated to wildlife habitats.

Quick succession relief

This is a scaled reduction of the tax payable on death where the deceased received chargeable transfers within five years before death. The tax is reduced by 80% where the transfer was made two years before death, 60% for three years, 40% for four years and 20% for five years.

Property sales

Where sales are made on or after 10 March 1993 of freehold or leasehold property, and the sale is made within 4 years after death (previously 3 years), the sale price may be substituted for the value at death for inheritance tax purposes.

9.9 RE-ARRANGEMENT OF ESTATES

Within two years after death the dispositions of an estate made by a will can be rearranged by the written agreement of all beneficiaries, and this could have the effect of reducing inheritance tax. In 1989/90 and onwards these rearrangements will only be effective for inheritance tax purposes where they make adequate provision for the dependants of the deceased.

9.10 GENERAL CONCLUSIONS

The foregoing is no more than a résumé of the essentials of this highly complex tax. Expert professional advice is of the greatest importance when taxpayers seek to mitigate this tax. Subject to proper advice, the tax can be relieved by such methods as: taking advantage of the annual exemptions for gifts, transfers to spouses and to charities, and the establishment of trusts for children and dependants. If the risk of dying within seven years is accepted, substantial gifts during lifetime instead of legacies at death may be appropriate.

APPENDIX

SELF-ASSESSMENT

The following is an edited extract from the Notes on Self-Assessment produced by The Vyner Group for use by purchasers of its "Simplex" accounts books and stationery.

1. THE NEW "SELF-ASSESSMENT" SYSTEM FOR TAXATION.

This new system started in April 1997 and is now in its second year of operation. The term "self-assessment" is a bit misleading, since those taxpayers who don't want to work out the actual tax bill themselves can ask the Inland Revenue to do it for them – but in that case they must send in the completed return by 30 September. From April to September is plenty of time to fill in the Tax Return, and you are strongly advised to complete the Return as soon as you have collected all the records you need to deal with it.

Payment of tax is made in three instalments: the first by 31 January in the tax year; the second by the following 31 July; and the final balance due on the following 31 January. The first two payments are equal to half of the total liability for the previous tax year. The final, balancing payment is based on the actual tax return for the year and the resulting assessment (either by the Inland Revenue or by Self-Assessment, whichever is applicable – see para 1 above). If you opt for Self-Assessment and the final return is not made by the deadline of 31 January following the tax year concerned, a £100 penalty is due in addition to any tax liability.

Unless your tax affairs are very complicated (i.e. you have different sources of income) it is unlikely you will need to seek professional advice, but of course you are free to do so if you wish. The Inland Revenue will be manning its telephone lines and tax advice centres to help those who are having difficulties.

2. HOW THE SELF-ASSESSMENT SYSTEM WORKS

At the end of the tax year, in April, you should have received from the Inland Revenue a tax form called the Tax Return 1998. This is a "user-friendly" tax form because it takes you through the whole self-assessment procedure step-by step. Accompanying the form is a Tax Return Guide which offers a great deal more information.

Page 1 of the Tax Return tells you about the new arrangements.

Page 2 tells you about the Supplementary Pages which must be completed by those who have certain types of income. By reading carefully through the information on Page 2 you can work out which of these supplementary pages apply to you. We reproduce below the questions you will be asked on this Page so that you can discover which Supplementary Pages you are going to need to fill in. The Inspector will have sent you most of them, but it is *your responsibility* to get any that have not been supplied. You can ring the Orderline on 0645-000404 to get any pages that you require.

Establishing which Supplementary Pages you need

1. Were you an employee, or office holder, or director, or agency worker in the year ended 5 April 1998?

   If yes, you need the Employment Pages

2. Did you have any taxable income from share options or share related benefits in the year?

   If yes, you need the Share Schemes Pages

3. Were you self-employed (but not in partnership)?

   If yes, you need the Self-Employment Pages

4. Were you in partnership?

   If yes, you need the Partnership Pages

5. Did you receive any rent or other income from land and property in the UK?

   If yes, you need the Land & Property Pages

6. Did you have any taxable income form overseas pensions or benefits, or from foreign companies or savings institutions, offshore funds or trusts abroad, or from land and property abroad or gains on foreign insurance policies?

   Have you at any time made, or been associated with, a transfer of assets which has resulted in income becoming payable to a foreign entity or have you benefited in any way from such a transfer made by someone else?

   Do you want to claim tax credit relief for foreign tax paid on foreign income or gains?

   If yes to any, you need the Foreign Pages

7. Did you receive any income from any trust, settlement or estate of a deceased person?

   If yes, you need the Trusts Etc. Pages

8. Capital gains:

(i) Have you disposed of your exempt only or main residence?

If "yes", read page 7 of your Tax Return Guide to see if you need the Capital Gains Pages.

(ii) Did you dispose of other chargeable assets worth more than £13 000 in total?

(iii) Were your chargeable gains more than £6 500?

If yes to either, you need the Capital Gains Pages

You may also need to fill in the Capital Gains Pages if you made a loss.

9. Are you claiming that you were not resident, or not ordinarily resident, or domiciled, in the UK, or dual resident in the UK and another country, for all or part of the year?

If yes, you need the Non-Residence Etc. Pages

Filling in the Supplementary Pages

In order to fill in the Supplementary Pages you will need to collect together all the information that you normally need to complete your tax return form every April. For example, in the case of the Employment Pages the chief piece of evidence is the P60 that you receive from your employer at the end of the tax year. This shows the total earnings, the tax deducted during the year and so on. For the Self Employment Pages (also called Schedule 3) and the Partnership Pages (also called Schedule 4) the chief evidence will be the accounts in which you have recorded the profits of your business.

The Tax Calculation Guide

The Inland Revenue will have sent you with your Tax Return a Tax Calculation Guide which you can use to calculate your tax once you have filled in the Supplementary Pages. You do not have to do your own Tax Calculation if you do not want to, but remember you must send your Tax Return by **30 September** if you wish the Inspector to complete your assessment for you.

The Tax Calculation Guide begins with a number of "W" boxes (W for Worksheet). You write in the W boxes the amount of income you have arrived at for each of the Supplementary Pages.

An example might be as follows (overleaf):

Total income from:		*Copy totals from the Supplementary Pages into this column*
Employment (see your P60)	W1	–
Share Schemes (Box 2.31)	W2	–
Self-employment (Box 3.88)	W3	£27 364.40
Partnership (Boxes 4.35, 4.70 and 4.73)	W4	–
Land and Property (Box 5.43)	W5	£2 360.00
Foreign income (Boxes 6.2, 6.4 and 6.5)	W6	–
Trust, settlements or estates of deceased persons	W7	–
UK savings and investments	W8	£1 742.60
UK pensions, retirement annuities, etc.	W9	–
Maintenance and alimony received (Box 12.3)	W10	–
Other income (Box 13.3 – Box 13.5)	W11	–
		£31,567.00

Figures on W7-9 will follow the notes given in the tax calculation form. However, you need only do this if you are doing your own calculation – if you send in your form by 30th September the Inland Revenue will complete this for you.

Once the figure for total income has been calculated, the rest of your Tax Return which is now concerned with the reliefs and allowances to which you are entitled, can be completed.

Before we look at this part of the Tax Return, we will first look at the completion of the Supplementary Pages for self-employed people who are *not* trading as a partnership.

Completing the Self-Employment Pages
(for those not trading as a partnership)

These make a 4-page document. The first page (SE1) simply asks for more details of your business.

1. Very small businesses (turnover less than £15 000)

The Self-Employment Pages contain a short section for very small businesses, with a turnover below £15,000. In these cases all the Inland Revenue asks for are simple three-line accounts (no details are required):

Takings – Expenses = Profits

An example might be:

Turnover, goods taken for personal use and other business receipts	£14 256
Expenses allowable for tax	£7 642
Net profit	£6 614

2. Businesses with turnover greater than £15 000

The first line of this section is important. It reads: "Tick either box 3.14 or box 3.15 if the figures used in your Final accounts (boxes 3.16-3.51) include VAT (3.14) or exclude VAT (3.15)". Once you have ticked the relevant box, complete the rest of the form. An example might be:

Sales/business income (turnover)	3.16		£52 740.40
Cost of Sales	3.33	£17 231.90	
Construction industry subcontractor costs	3.34	—	
Other direct costs	3.35	—	
Total costs (3.33+3.34+3.35)			£17 251.90
(Box 3.16 less boxes 3.33+3.34+3.35)	3.36		£35 488.50
Other income/profits	3.37		£850.20

Expenditure

Employee costs	3.38	£4,575.52	
Premises costs	3.39	£1,764.40	
Repairs	3.40	£458.23	
General administrative expenses	3.41	£325.60	
Motor expenses	3.42	£625.35	
Travel and subsistence	3.43	—	
Advertising, promotion and entertainment	3.44	£100.00	
Legal and professional costs	3.45	£78.00	
Bad debts	3.46	—	
Interest	3.47	—	
Other finance charges	3.48	£484.60	
Depreciation and loss/(profit) on sale	3.49	£562.60	
Other expenditure	3.50	—	
Total expenses	3.51		£8 974.30
Net profit (box 3.36 + box 3.37 – box 3.51)	3.52		£26 364.40

Note: Boxes 3.17-3.32 have been left out of this example. They deal with disallowable expenses, and adjust the profits slightly. They are explained in the Self Employment Pages.

3. Entering VAT information

If you are *not* registered for VAT all the figures entered in both sales (box 3.16) and expenses (boxes 3.33-3.51) are gross of VAT and there is no need to take any further action about VAT. Just work out your net profit as shown.

If you *are* registered for VAT you have to take some special actions:

(i) If you are an ordinary trader (not dealing in zero-rated goods) the VAT in relation to revenue (non-capital) items paid over in the year to

Customs & Excise must appear as “Other Expenditure” in box 3.50. (Do not include any VAT refunds relating to capital expenditures – these can be stripped out by adding back the total VAT recovered on such expenditure to the total amount paid over in the year to Customs and Excise.)

(ii) If you are a trader in zero-rated goods and receive refunds of VAT, the amount of the refunds in relation to revenue (non-capital) items must be included in “Other Income” in box 3.37. (Do not include any VAT refunds relating to capital expenditures – these can be stripped out by deducting the total VAT recovered on such expenditure from the total amount refunded by Customs and Excise.)

The remaining sides of the Self-Employment Pages are adjustments of your net profit or loss to take account of a variety of minor points. There are Help sheets available on some of these points, and the Inland Revenue advice lines and its Tax Centres will be able to answer any of your queries.

Completing the Partnership Pages

If you are a partner in a partnership business, one of the partners is responsible for completing the Partnership Pages and the final result will give you the total profit of your partnership business. This has to be shared among the partners in the agreed way (see pages 6 and 7 of the Partnership Tax Return) and copies must be given to each partner so he/she can complete his/her SA Tax Return 1998.

Other Supplementary Pages

When the other Supplementary Pages which you are affected by have been completed, you can complete the income section of the Self-Assessment Return (Q11-13), and you can also complete the Total income section of your Tax Calculation Guide to show your Total Income from all sources.

Deductions and allowances

Having completed the Income part of the Self Assessment Return (Q11-13), the next part of the Return (Q14-16) simply continues with the various deductions and allowances to which you are entitled. These adjust the tax payable to take account of your personal situation, whatever it may be. First complete Q14-16 in the Tax Return and then transfer the data to the Tax Calculation Guide as indicated in the Guide to work out the actual amount of tax payable (unless you return your form before 30 September, in which case the Inspector will do the calculation for you).

Completion of your Tax Return

To complete the Self-Assessment, answer Q17 in the Tax Return, then transfer the data from your completed Tax Calculation Guide to the relevant parts of Q18 and Q19 of the Tax Return (as indicated in the Tax Calculation Guide), and complete the rest of the Tax Return as instructed.

Note to readers: Every effort has been made to ensure that the advice given in this book is correct, but we regret we cannot accept any liability for errors arising from the use of these notes. Your Tax Return must be based on the official forms sent to you by the Inland Revenue, and their Official Guides and Help Sheets.

INDEX

Standing Order for

TAXATION SIMPLIFIED

To: Management Books 2000 Ltd
Cowcombe House
Cowcombe Hill
Chalford
Glos GL6 8HP

Please forward me a copy of
TAXATION SIMPLIFIED
together with an invoice
on publication until further notice

Name ....

Address..

....

....

Signature...

PLEASE Photocopy